To Touch Inward Springs

To Touch Inward Springs

Teaching and Learning for Faith Development

BETTY JO MIDDLETON

TO TOUCH INWARD SPRINGS
TEACHING AND LEARNING FOR FAITH DEVELOPMENT

iUniverse books may be ordered through booksellers or by contacting:

iUniverse
1663 Liberty Drive
Bloomington, IN 47403
www.iuniverse.com
1-800-Authors (1-800-288-4677)

Because of the dynamic nature of the Internet, any web addresses or links contained in this book may have changed since publication and may no longer be valid. The views expressed in this work are solely those of the author and do not necessarily reflect the views of the publisher, and the publisher hereby disclaims any responsibility for them.

Any people depicted in stock imagery provided by Thinkstock are models, and such images are being used for illustrative purposes only.
Certain stock imagery © Thinkstock.

ISBN: 978-1-4917-7358-1 (sc)
ISBN: 978-1-4917-7357-4 (e)

Library of Congress Control Number: 2015913341

Print information available on the last page.

iUniverse rev. date: 09/03/2015

Also by Betty Jo Middleton

The 4U History Book Club. Year One
*While You're Growing: Strategies and Resources for Small Religious
    Education Programs*
Support for the Volunteer Religious Education Teacher
Special Times: Honoring Our Jewish and Christian Heritages
First Steps: Planning for Adult Religious Education. A Process Guide
Celebrating Our Roots and Branches
With Frank Robertson and Others: *World Religions for Junior Youth*
    (Kit)

This book is dedicated to my family,
learners and teachers all

Publication of *To Touch Inward Springs* is made possible by a generous grant from the Unitarian Sunday School Society.

Contents

The great end in religious instruction, whether in the Sunday-school or the family, is, not to stamp *our* minds irresistibly on the young, but to stir up their own; not to make them see with our eyes, but to look inquiringly and steadily with their own; not to give them a definite amount of knowledge, but to inspire a fervent love of truth; not to form an outward regularity, but to touch inward springs; not to burden the memory but to quicken and strengthen the power of thought; not to bind them by ineradicable prejudices to our particular sect or peculiar notions, but to prepare them to impartial conscientious judging of whatever subjects may, in the course of Providence, be offered to their decision; not to impose religion upon them in the form of arbitrary rules, which rest on no foundation but our own words and will, but to awaken the consciousness, the moral discernment, so that they may discern and approve for themselves what is everlastingly good and right.

—William Ellery Channing, 1837

Preface

Teaching and learning have been important to me at every stage of my life. The household I grew up in was truly a learning laboratory. My mother had taught in a mixed age elementary classroom before her first child was born; she supplemented all of our learning with crafts, books, games, and toys at home. She even taught us gymnastics. Our kitchen experiences included making paste from flour and water. We learned about fractions by measuring ingredients for baking. My father was skilled at carpentry and, in addition to making a child-sized ironing board and furniture, doll beds, and wooden trains, built for us an outdoor playground. It started with a playhouse, but went on to include a wooden airplane the size of a Piper Cub, a seesaw, a zip line, and a flying jenny—a marvelous makeshift contraption that looked like a seesaw but functioned like a merry-go-round, consisting of a board attached to a wagon wheel, mounted on a low post in the ground, and powered by a child who pushed the board to get it started whirling and then jumped onto it. In addition to free play and physical exercise, this equipment helped us learn to deal with social situations, as the backyard was usually full of children from other families as well as our own. Our life was not idyllic, but we did have lots of fun.

As a child I enjoyed a somewhat eclectic religious upbringing, I learned a little of the Roman Catholic catechism from Maria,

Theresa, and Leona Kraesig at my grandmother's house one Sunday each month; on other Sundays we attended the Methodist Church School. In addition, we had family prayers and Bible reading every evening. At other times of the day we might hear one of our parents singing "It Ain't Necessarily So" from *Porgy and Bess*, which cast some doubt on "things that you're liable to read in the Bible." We learned to take Holy Writ seriously, but not too seriously. I enjoyed it all!

I was a child who liked school, too. I started first grade in 1939, during the heyday of the Progressive Movement. Our public elementary school classrooms each had a sand table, providing opportunities for learning through play. The first and second graders sat in child size chairs at low tables. One first grade teacher assigned work with Roman Numerals to more advanced students, while the others caught up. The third and fourth grade room had fixed desks, but small groups gathered on the recitation bench in the front of the room or worked in the adjacent cloakroom. Often one student would tutor another sitting in the hallway outside the classroom. Stereopticon slides (already an archaic novelty) provided visual interest in history and geography, while a repository of objects from nature gave us first hand knowledge and tactile experience as we handled them. We visited the shop classroom for simple woodworking projects. Teachers read aloud every day, introducing us to literature as a significant and pleasant part of our routine. First and second graders had a rhythm band. We sang in regular assemblies. And at the end of the school year everyone in the elementary school appeared onstage in an operetta. Not a cast of thousands, but of about seventy-five.

Early on I became aware of differences in teaching, although it was many years before I realized how many factors were involved: content, setting, space restrictions, as well as teaching styles, each teacher's understanding of how people learn, and what activities might be useful in teaching. At our church Mrs. Waldrep's primary class met in the choir loft, sitting on low benches at a long table that provided space for both artwork and for the picture cards that served as attendance records, to which we affixed stickers each Sunday. One I recall had a scene of Jesus in a meadow, and—a special delight—the stickers were little sheep. Each of the other teachers had a church pew for a classroom, somewhat restricting the range of activities. When my cousin Kathryn taught in the Vacation Church School, she introduced chancel drama, block building, and other activities to the program. When we spatter painted leaves, using old toothbrushes, wire screening, and a bit of paint, I had an experience akin to that of Annie Dillard who reports being "shocked to the core" when she folded paper into little geese at the Unitarian church she visited with her friend Judy.[1] Such experiences serve to keep the sense of wonder alive, or to awaken it when it has become dulled by lack of encouragement and use.

As a teenager, I taught in the Vacation Church School. After high school graduation, I worked in the school office and was a substitute teacher at every grade level. During my college years, I did educational work in rural Methodist churches in Arkansas, at camps and conferences, and in a local congregation. Before preparing for the Ministry of Religious Education, many years later, I was a volunteer teacher in three Unitarian Universalist congregations. There I found teacher's guides to the books in the New Beacon Series were informative and helpful. Later I taught preschool for two years. I have taught religious education classes for all ages, as well as courses at two theological schools. At every stage I have been aware of the importance of learning about teaching in order to do it better. This book is a result of my continuing efforts to learn all that I can about the subject at hand, and to share that learning with others.

Acknowledgements

This book would not have been written without the encouragement, support, gentle critique, and wise counsel of my friend and colleague Margaret Corletti. Marge read it all, portions of it many times as I continued to write and rewrite, and offered fresh insight at every draft. I am deeply grateful.

My husband Howard was my "first reader" and he, too, read many drafts as a kind and helpful critic and helped me to clarify my thinking and my writing. My friend and neighbor Joelle Dolas read it with an editor's eye and her suggestions resulted in many improvements. My daughter Lucia read many chapters and my son Jay read portions and helped me with references. Many thanks to each of them.

The Unitarian Sunday School Society gave me a grant that made publication possible and the Mount Vernon Unitarian Church served as fiscal agent. Richard Gilbert was helpful in providing information about publishing with iUniverse. I am grateful to them all.

In a long life of learning I have had many formally designated teachers, and I am grateful to them, as well as to family and friends who have been my teachers. I am especially grateful to those with whom I have taught and/or designed seminary courses: Marge (again), Linda Olson Peebles, Ginger Luke, Judith Mannheim, the late Roberta M. Nelson, and the late Eugene B. Navias; those with whom I designed Renaissance Module leader's guides: Abby L.W. Crowley, Elizabeth Boyd Stevens, Gene Navias (again), Elizabeth Curtis, Alice Blair Wesley, and Gaia Brown; the many who co-led Renaissance Modules with me, and the students and participants in classes and modules.

When I posted requests for information, responses came almost immediately from Christina Leone Tracy, Linda Weaver, Carla Miller, Lara Profitt, Karen Scrivo, Helen Zidowecki, Deborah Bernaka, Cathy Cartwright-Chow, Kate Sullivan, Morgan Watson, and Beth Brownfield. Elizabeth Motander Jones, Elizabeth Strong, and Richard Kimball responded in detail to questions I posed. Elizabeth Katzmann and Meg Riley gave me permission to use their Rainbow Path principles in Chapter Fifteen. I am truly grateful.

Despite all of this help, I alone am responsible for any errors.

Introduction

This is a book about teaching for faith development. Although written from a Unitarian Universalist perspective it draws on many sources. It touches on various aspects of religious education, but the primary focus is pedagogy—teaching approaches, methods, and learning activities appropriate and effective for faith development in persons of all ages. By faith development I mean a person's growing and evolving engagement with and commitment to life, a person's relationship with self, others, and the universe.

We have all grown accustomed to the term "R.E." being used almost universally among us for "religious education," and often really meaning, "the children's program of the church." I use the term "religious education" to mean programs designed for teaching and learning for faith development, for any and all ages, but not to mean faith development itself. Sometimes I use "religious growth and learning programs" to mean the same as "religious education." The words "model," "method," and "learning theory" are used with different meanings by different people and often interchangeably. I hope that I have made clear distinctions between them, using "model" only in the sense of structural models for organizing programs, "method" with the time honored meaning of how we teach, and "learning theory" for ideas about how people learn. I use the words "youth" and "teens" interchangeably.

This work is intended for all who have a sincere interest in teaching and learning for faith development, including but not limited to teachers, lifespan religious education committee members, students for ministry and religious education, religious educators, and ministers. The importance of the role of the teacher was recognized early on. William Ellery Channing, in his 1837 *Discourse* to the Sunday School Society, said "Like all schools, the Sunday-school must owe its influence to its teachers ... the most gifted in our congregations cannot find a worthier field of labor than the Sunday-school."[2] The importance of the volunteer teacher to the religious education enterprise continues to be recognized. Indeed, most adults when asked about childhood religious education experiences, report that they remember a *teacher*, as distinct from any specific experience.

No method or approach is as important as the character and the commitment, the personhood, of the teacher. Parker Palmer writes, "good teaching cannot be reduced to technique; good teaching comes from the identity and integrity of the teacher."[3] Yet development as a teacher is enhanced by learning about approaches, methods, and activities appropriate to lifespan faith development in the liberal church. Religious educators have a teaching role with teachers, parents, and others in the congregation; their understanding of the processes of learning and teaching is critical. Teaching is a significant aspect of ministry, whether in the pulpit, the counseling room, the community, the classroom, or working with religious education volunteers. It is my hope that people in each of these groups— teachers, religious educators, and ministers—will find this work useful.

My enthusiasm is for learning that is experiential, participatory, conversational, cooperative, and creative; that is reflected throughout the book. In my many years of teaching in religious education programs and of working with teachers, I have found these methods to be most effective.

The book is in two parts. Part One consists of foundational material for methodology discussed in Part Two. The first chapter provides a historical and philosophical background for the book. The title, "The Transient and Permanent in Religious Education," pays homage to, as well as plays on and with, the title of a significant work in Unitarian Universalism. Theodore Parker's controversial 1841 *Discourse on the Transient and Permanent in Christianity* scandalized many of the Unitarian clergy of its day, but it has inspired many variations on the theme. One was the 1995 convocation of Unitarian Universalist ministers and the subsequent book inspired by the proceedings. Parker said "… in that portion of Christianity which is preached and believed—there seem to have been, ever since the time of its earthly founder, two elements, the one transient, the other permanent. The one is the thought, the folly, the uncertain wisdom, the theological notions, the impiety of man; the other, the eternal truth of God. These two bear the same relation to each other that the phenomena of outward nature, such as sunshine and cloud, growth, decay, and reproduction, bear to the great law of nature, which underlies and supports them all. As in that case, more attention is commonly paid to the particular phenomena than to the general law; so in this case, more is generally given to the Transient in Christianity than to the Permanent therein. It must be confessed, though with sorrow, that transient things form a great part of what is commonly taught as Religion."[4]

In *The Transient and Permanent in Liberal Religion*, Dan O'Neal writes that Parker "asked and answered a very simple but important question about the Unitarianism of his day: What was permanent and enduring about that movement as it attempted to address the needs and conditions of the age in which it lived; and what was transient, tied to passing beliefs and circumstances, and therefore not to be held onto tightly?... The arrival of a new millennium is an appropriate time to look at the transient and permanent in present-day Unitarian Universalism. This book is an attempt by contemporary UU observers to do just that."[5]

Richard Fewkes, in the guise of Theodore Parker, wrote in 1995 (in more contemporary and concise language) "… I endeavored to show that the theologies and doctrines about Christ were transient and changeable from one generation to another, while his moral teachings of love to God and love to humankind were permanent and true whether he ever spoke them or not. Even if he never existed, his teachings were still true. This is the gist of what I said and even many of my more conservative Unitarian colleagues seemed courteous and well disposed to my remarks."[6]

Despite efforts to "un-school" religious education over the years, the idea that our work is primarily to transmit information persists in some quarters. Considering the purpose of programs for faith development will help us to consider other methods. This is discussed in the second chapter, "Nurturing the Spirit."

Chapters Three and Four make up a section on how people learn. Theories of learning, with a special emphasis on Multiple Intelligences, are the focus of Chapter Three. Chapter Four examines some of the factors inherent in practice—human development, identity, differences, and diversity. I have experienced on more than one occasion the gap between intent and result in the classroom. This chapter grows out of my own learnings in order to lessen, if not close, that gap.

The next two chapters focus on teaching. Chapter Five covers approaches to teaching, including text-centered, teacher-centered, child-centered, subject-centered, shared praxis, showing how, discovery and inquiry, and teaching for understanding. I include the "Montessori approach" in this chapter, although it is generally referred to as the "Montessori Method." This structured, ordered approach to religious education may utilize any number of methods. It is discussed along with contemporary programs such as Jerome Berryman's Godly Play and Bonita Penfold's Spirit Play. Chapter Six identifies and describes seven categories of teaching methods I propose for use in programs of religious growth and learning. A chapter on each method is found in Part Two.

The third section of Part One covers organization of the program. Chapter Seven focuses on models and structures we use in designing programs for use in the liberal community of faith. This is a topic I have dealt with elsewhere, most notably in "How We Do What We Do in Religious Education,"[7] but with one important change. At that time I included "Educating Community" as one of the models under use or discussion among us, but I have since concluded that it is now a significant part of our philosophy. The structural models discussed are: classroom based, home and family education, religious education without walls, rotation, and worship-education. Structures for youth and adult programming are included as well. Chapter Eight is on mixed age groupings and multigenerational learning. By "Sunday morning" or "Sunday morning program" I mean the primary worship/gathering hour for the congregation, be it actually Sunday morning, Wednesday evening, Saturday afternoon or some other time.

Part Two includes a chapter on each of seven teaching methods identified in Chapter Seven. These are: storytelling and other presentations that engage participants, creative expression opportunities, play—and its significance in the development of faith, discourse —conversation, discussion, questions, centers or stations for learning, real world experiences such as field trips and social justice projects, and reflection and meditation. A variety of learning activities are suggested. Learning goals, discipline, preparing to teach, and the relationship between content and methodology are discussed.

The final chapter is "Tomorrow's Children and Today's Heritage," paying homage to another significant book. The philosophy of the New Beacon Series of religious education curriculum was put forth in Sophia Lyon Fahs' book *Today's Children and Yesterday's Heritage,*[8] published in 1952. In this chapter attention is given to planning programs for the future. I suggest a more flexible, inclusive model for Sunday morning programs, family designed learning, and full week emphasis on religious education. Social media and computer learning are discussed.

Attention is given to the role of technology. Even as electronic and digital communication becomes ubiquitous and new methods of learning emerge, people gathering together in groups becomes more important. This book is for such times.

PART ONE

Chapter One

The Transient and Permanent in Religious Education

"What is the core of our evolving Unitarian Universalist faith?"
—Essex Coordinating Committee

I first thought of asking the question "What is transient and what is permanent in religious education?" when I came across a twenty-five year old outline for a religious education workshop and realized that if I were leading the workshop that day, there were many things that I would not change at all. I wondered if I had learned nothing in those twenty-five years of working as a religious educator. Further reflection led me to think about the significance of what had changed, and what had not.

Religious education is comparatively new as a field of study and as a profession.

Mary Boys, Catholic educator and intellectual historian, dates its beginning to the 1830s, with the publication of Congregationalist Horace Bushnell's *Christian Nurture* and Unitarian William Ellery Channing's *Discourse Pronounced Before the Sunday School Society*.[9] She defines religious education as "a classic expression that weds classic liberal theology and progressivist educational thought."[10]

Writing in the 1980s, Boys says *"Religious education ...* encompasses Channing's Unitarianism, Bushnell's preference for nurture within the family over adolescent conversion, and the Dewey-Coe-Elliott commitment to education as reconstruction. These elements have continued through the present day in the educational commitments of the Unitarian Universalist church and its 'cousin' traditions, such as the Ethical Culture Society; in the work of the Religious Experience Research Unit at Manchester College, Oxford; and in the work of Paulo Freire and Gabriel Moran."[11] It is interesting to note that Moran says "religious education is a term of self-description for only a few groups, such as British schoolteachers, Catholic Directors of Religious Education in the United States, and Unitarian educators."[12]

In 1999, when the Liberal Religious Educators Association (LREDA) celebrated the Fiftieth Anniversary of its founding, the history of religious education was presented at the Fall Conference in Plymouth, Massachusetts. Talks covered four eras: The Early Years, The Fahs/MacLean Era, An Era of Change, and The RE Futures Era. Elizabeth Strong has suggested that the "Early Years" be divided into two eras, the Catechetical being the first.[13] I refer to the second as the Early Curriculum Era, and to the "Era of Change" as the Kit Era. The current era (as of 2015) is referred to as Tapestry of Faith.

There have been changes throughout the years in what we do, and what we are trying to do, in educating for faith development. I became a Unitarian in 1958, and a Unitarian Universalist by virtue of consolidation of the American Unitarian Association (AUA) with the Universalist Church of America (UCA) in 1961. Thus have I experienced a few of the changes heralded as new eras. Each era has had its own rationale or philosophy, curriculum, primary method, and critique.

Catechetical Era: 1700s to 1800s

Pre-dating the 1830s, the primary mode of religious instruction was the catechism. Both Unitarians and Universalists used them. The rationale was simple: in order for children to be religious, they needed to memorize rote answers to questions about Biblical material. "The religious instruction of children in the faith of their ancestors was a high priority for the community and deeply imbedded in practice in the colonial period of America," according to Strong.[14] Although Judith Sargent Murray wrote the first known catechism for Universalists, published in 1782,[15] most were written by male clergy.

The critique of the catechism came from many, perhaps most colorfully from Channing in his *Discourse* in 1837. The catechism, he said, "is a skeleton, a dead letter, a petrification." The familiar part of the *Discourse* is more forward looking, but, as Eugene Navias has noted, although Channing's address was printed and widely read "there is no evidence that anyone tried to apply it to the development of curriculum or to teaching methods, until well in the 20th Century."[16]

Early Curriculum Era: 1830s to 1930s

The Sunday School Society —Unitarian was added to the name in 1868—published five curriculum series between 1833 and 1909, before transferring functions of teacher training and publishing Sunday school materials to the Department of Religious Education of the AUA. The Society (USSS) continues to support religious education work through its grants program, including publication of this book.

Both Unitarians and Universalists "participated in the International Uniform Lessons System from the 1870s to 1912. The Bible was the sole resource acceptable for use in the Sunday Schools by the American Sunday School Union, and from the beginnings in 1824, the method of teaching was through memorization, even in the lessons graded for the very young."[17] Both bodies published Helpers, to assist the teachers in making them somewhat more appropriate for learners, says Strong.

Progressive education, the organization of the Religious Education Association (REA), and cultural changes around the beginning of the twentieth century led to changes in approach and methodology for both Unitarians and Universalists. The influence of John Dewey was undeniable. Edward Horton was elected president of the Unitarian Sunday School Society in 1892. David Parke writes that this "marked the beginning of the modern era in Unitarian religious education...When it ended eighteen years later, the progressives had all but won the day, and a curriculum incorporating progressive principles was already in use in Unitarian churches."[18]

The Beacon Series was created. Publication of the Universalist Murray Graded Series, reflecting Higher Criticism of the Bible, progressive education ideas, and evolutionary theory, lasted from 1912 into the 1930s. The rationale in the early years of this era (1830s and forward) was pretty much the same as that of the Catechetical Era: transmitting prescribed knowledge. As the century progressed, correctives began to emerge to meet the primary critique: that it was not age appropriate.

Fahs/MacLean Era 1930–1965

The philosophy for this era was summed up in Sophia Fahs' book *Today's Children and Yesterday's Heritage*, with an introduction by Angus MacLean. The book was published in 1952, more than halfway through the Era. Fahs described a child's religion as "a vital and healthy result" of the child's creative thought and feeling and experience in response to the fullness of life, laying the groundwork for a methodology based on experience and reflection.[19]

MacLean was a sensitive and imaginative teacher of religious education at St. Lawrence Theological School, where almost all ministerial students also were qualified as religious educators. He is known for *The Method is the Message*, given as an address to the Universalist Sabbath School Union of Boston. It was later expanded by MacLean and published by the UUA.[20]

The New Beacon Series, the curriculum for this era, consisted of books for children and youth accompanied by guides for teachers and parents, pamphlets, leaflets, and other resources. These included the *Martin and Judy* books for preschool and kindergarten children, books about babies, family life, Jesus, nature, science, and venturing out into the world for elementary children; Unitarian Universalism, "great men" such as Abraham and Moses, Socrates, and Akhenaten. A perennial favorite was *The Church Across the Street* for junior and senior high. Authors for these materials included Fahs, MacLean, Dorothy Spoerl, Elizabeth and Reginald Manwell, Charles C. Forman, Edith Hunter, Josephine Gould, and Bertha Stevens.

The method involved the use of stories and a variety of experiential exercises, especially for younger children. The work of religious education in churches and fellowships was supported by publications, workshops, and field workers sent out by both bodies.

Soon after the formation of the Unitarian Universalist Association six Commissions studied every aspect of this new institution. They made recommendations for the future which were published as a book, *The Free Church in a Changing World*. Commission III studied "Education and Liberal Religion." Its critique of the New Beacon Series and the work of the UUA in religious education informed the next era. Recommendations were concerned with both content and method. "Because we must not neglect religion as culture, the Bible should be taught in our Church Schools, and church history, and the history of religions" was one.[21] Another related to the guides accompanying the books. "The very methods used in our Church Schools hold us to the recognition of [the] priority of immediate, personal religious experience as over against historical, organized religion."[22] Most of the Teachers' Guides, though, were found wanting and the Commission gave detailed instructions for revision.

The report noted that materials were not realistic in presenting only one social strata, that of middle class children living in the suburbs.[23] While race was not mentioned in the report, a critique from the field was the lack of racial diversity in the materials. Several books for young children, with illustrations reflecting minimal racial diversity, were added to the curriculum as a result. The Commission noted also that our "child-centered approach and experiential methodology should not blind us to the need of Unitarian Universalist boys and girls for specific learnings." But, it went on, "We do *not* want a content-centered curriculum. We shall continue to emphasize the fact that in a very real sense the method *is* the message."[24]

Other critiques were by Robert Miller and Dorothy Spoerl. Miller advocated "a radical revision of the teacher's guides with more focus on the growing experiences of young people in their own lives, a broader approach to the study of religious beliefs and traditions, and more democratic structuring of agendas in classrooms."[25] In Spoerl's paper, written in 1962, she compared it with previous curricula. Her purpose was to point out the advances that had been made in curriculum development and to emphasize that the writers of the New Beacon Series viewed their books, guides, and other materials as an ongoing process, always to be added to as an expanding body of resources for teachers, parents, and young people, and open to continuing research and revision."[26] Frank Robertson says that she "reaffirmed the influence of progressive education on curricula and concluded 'teachers and children together, growing into an awareness of the spiritual meanings of living—this is the genius of the New Beacon Series in Religious Education.'"[27]

The Commission had noted that materials for younger children were more adequate than those for middle childhood. "In developing concepts necessary for every day life, our curriculum neglects philosophy and theology.... In forming attitudes toward social groups and institutions, too little attention is paid to social problems and institutions, including the Unitarian Universalist church."[28] This lack of emphasis on Unitarian Universalism continued throughout the Kit Era and was much criticized.

The Unitarian Education Directors Association, now Liberal Religious Educators Association (LREDA), was formed in 1949 in order to set and achieve standards for professional religious educators.

The Kit Era 1965–1980

Hugo Hollerorth became curriculum director for the UUA in 1965, ushering in the era of multi-media kits. The eighteen curriculum kits produced during this era contained leaders' guides, books, learning games, audio-visual aids, background material for leaders, and sometimes other items.

Describing "a bold new adventure in curriculum development" that had emerged from a revolution in education, Hollerorth said that the goals of this new effort are "To help children discover ideas and concepts with which to understand and cope with experience; to aid them in developing their powers of perception and critical thinking; to nurture within them certain attitudes and sensitivities and help them acquire certain social skills."[29]

Kits were developed for people of all ages, kindergarten through adults. Only two were for young children; one of these, *The Haunting House*, was especially beloved by children, teachers, and religious educators. The *About Your Sexuality (AYS)* program for junior high youth was both appreciated and controversial.

One hallmark of this era was the excellent and unprecedented teacher training program; as each kit was developed, teachers were trained to conduct the field test, and as it went into production, trainers were selected to train teachers throughout the UUA. After the first round of trainings, this was generally dropped, except for *The Haunting House* and *AYS*. Prior training remained a requirement for teaching *AYS* as it does for teaching *Our Whole Lives (OWL)*, the current human sexuality program. Suggestions from field test teachers were often incorporated into the finished product. One example is the Harriet Tubman session in *The Adventures of God's Folk*, developed by teachers at All Souls Church in Washington, DC. The creation of this session was in response to the lack of women and people of color in the curriculum.

The primary method used was that of discovery, and later, inquiry. Hollerorth recognized the importance of the spiral curriculum, which revisits subjects at different levels throughout the life span, and had earlier been recommended by Commission III.

The Kit curriculum had detractors as well as supporters. One critique from the field was the cost of the kits; another was the lack of emphasis on Unitarian Universalism, or for that matter, any specific religious content. The UUA responded to criticism with the Religion Making program, which offered suggestions for religious educators to highlight religious aspects which were in the kits but not identified as such. As always, congregations were free to supplement or substitute for the kits.

The most comprehensive critique was by Elizabeth Holden Baker, in an address to the UU Advance Conference in Washington, DC, in 1980. Having discussed all previous eras of curriculum development, Baker said, "I am unable to see a coherent educational philosophy in the Multi-Media Curriculum Units. In each of the preceding curricula we have been able to trace the prevailing schools of thought." Baker also noted, that "in the last fifteen years the denomination has produced only seven kits for children under fourteen. The result is that individual churches are trying with dubious success to create or find materials they can use."[30]

In addition to adapting materials, congregations and individuals created their own; some were published through the UUA's REACH packet. Locally created materials used throughout the movement were those of Unity Church, Unitarian, St. Paul, MN; First Parish Church, Weston, MA; and the Joseph Priestley District Religious Education Committee. The Unity curriculum *Images for Our Lives* was later published by the UUA.

One last kit, not of the Kit Era, was published in 1985: *World Religions for Junior Youth*, created by a team headed by Robertson. This kit straddled two eras and had characteristics of each. One notable addition was the clearly stated Goals for Participants.

John Westerhoff's socialization or enculturation theory, reminding us of Bushnell's concept of nurture, was a strong influence. Jean Starr Williams and others wrote about "The Reaching Place" as an improvement on religious education classes. James Fowler's theory of faith development influenced religious educators to look at yet another aspect of human development when planning programs.

The UUA's Accreditation Program for religious educators, with preparation through an Independent Study Program, was established near the end of this era.

The Futures Era 1980–1999

The development of the multi-media kits coincided with the anti-schooling school reform movement and social tumult of the Sixties. Times changed, and as "Back to Basics" became the byword for secular education, the UUA moved into a new era. A group of Unitarian Universalist leaders had met for a series of presentations and discussion to help plan for the future. Each participant answered these questions in writing:

- What is Unitarian Universalism?
- What are the objectives of Unitarian Universalist Religious Education?
- What content and experiences should be included in our curriculum to fulfill these objectives?

The responses were published in *Stone House Conversations* "to assist congregations in resolving some of the disagreements and controversies which hinder the development of religious education programs to which they can give their enthusiastic support."[31]

A Religious Education Futures Committee was established and after a thorough process of gathering opinions and data published its report in 1981. "As education is a process of becoming, religious education is a process which nurtures religious becoming. 'Religious growth,' and 'faith development' are terms which describe the end-in-view of the religious education process." It called for curricula to "embody and identify Unitarian Universalist principles."[32] No other recommendation of the Committee was carried out with such zeal.

Elizabeth Anastos and David Marshak, Coordinators of Curriculum Development, created a process for congregations to use in planning for religious growth and learning. Published in 1984, *Philosophy-Making* offered a "detailed plan with several implementation options, for creating a philosophy of religious growth and learning for your society."[33]

A new spiral curriculum series, consisting of loosely graded programs created by teams formed regionally, was published. In all, fourteen guides to programs for children and youth were produced, with others for adults. All had elements focusing on Unitarian Universalist identity.

The influence of non-Unitarian Universalist religious educators was important in this era, especially Roman Catholics Maria Harris and Thomas Groome. Two of Harris' books were used as readers for the Renaissance program. Groome brought shared praxis to our attention. This approach informed the methodology of the Futures Era and has continued into Tapestry of Faith. Both Harris and Groome were Fahs Lecturers.

Issues of social justice became a major concern of religious education. Roberta Nelson and Richard Gilbert presented theme talks on *Religious Education and Social Action: Branches of the Same Tree* at the 1984 Unitarian Universalist National Workshop on Social Justice. These were later published in booklet form.[34] *In Our Hands*, a curriculum program for ages six through adult, with an emphasis on social justice, was published.

Beginning in the Futures Era and extending into the Tapestry Era was the development of *Our Whole Lives (OWL),* a human sexuality program with lesson plans for different age groups, kindergarten to adult. The program was developed by a task force representing the UUA and the United Church of Christ Board of Homeland Ministries. Publications for this program began in 1999 and continued into 2014. This replaced *About Your Sexuality.*

The Futures Committee Report had advocated support for independent curriculum developers, and their materials were recognized and publicized by the UUA. Among them were Mary Ann Moore, the Unitarian Universalist Christian Fellowship (UUCF), Brotman-Marshfield. Unitarian Universalist Curriculum and Resource Developers (UUCARDS) was organized. Wide spread use of these materials resulted in a less than coherent philosophy among congregations and no consistent methodology.

The recognition of the Ministry of Religious Education led to the Independent Study Program becoming preparation for that ministry. The Renaissance Program, with modular training components covering many aspects of religious education, was then created.

Tapestry of Faith 2000–the Present

Two gatherings of religious leaders at Essex House resulted in the publication of *Essex Conversations*, an introduction to a new era in religious education. Participants were asked to "imagine and articulate the core of Unitarian Universalist religious education… from various perspectives." The result was truly varied and did not offer a singular philosophy for the time to come.[35]

The primary distinguishing characteristic of this era is the posting of the Tapestry of Faith curriculum online at the UUA website, free to all. The program is described on the website this way: "Tapestry of Faith programs and resources for all ages are designed to nurture Unitarian Universalist identity, spiritual growth, a transforming faith, and vital communities of justice and love. This project developed out of a broad series of conversations that articulated a future direction for Unitarian Universalist religious growth and learning. In use since 2008 and continually evolving, Tapestry of Faith offers a variety of resources—downloadable, printed, viewable, interactive, and more—a religious growth and learning program for the 21st century."[36]

The curriculum is rich with stories, many of which are used in children's and multigenerational worship as well as in the classroom. Shared praxis has been a continued emphasis. There are programs for mixed-age classes and multigenerational groups, as well as more closely graded ones for children, youth programs, and classes intended for adults. The primary critique from users seems to be the sheer volume of materials. When printed they fill huge binders. Religious educators report winnowing down the lessons for teachers.

The idea of the congregation as an educating community has taken hold in the movement, evoking memories of the Reaching Place, enculturation, and Christian nurture. Multigenerational programming is an example of this influence.

The UUA's Credentialing Program for Religious Educators was established.

Transient and Permanent 1837–the Present

Parker reflected with sorrow that the transient—ideas insignificant in the long run—made up what was taught as Christianity. We may rejoice that in religious education we are able to let go of much that—even though once significant—is no longer pertinent for us, and to try new ways to implement the permanent. In fact, we may let go of something that might prove to be permanently valuable, for the sake of embracing the new. We have seen that old methodologies, specific curriculum, various credentialing practices, leaders (who, however important to their time and place, may be little remembered by the next generation of practitioners), and other aspects of religious education practice have been transient and have faded away.

The idea that education for faith should be experiential, developmental, and age appropriate has been with us since the days of Channing, as an ideal even when not practiced. The importance of the teacher was noted by Channing, Commission III on "Education and Liberal Religion," in the teaching helps provided by the AUA, Universalist groups, and the UUA, in the intensive training programs of the Multi-Media Kit Era, and in writings by Roberta Nelson, Barry Andrews, and others on teachers as spiritual guides. The increasing professionalism of religious educators through a variety of credentialing efforts has been a constant since the 1940s at least. LREDA has undergone many changes and in 2015 is a vibrant, broadly inclusive, engaged community of religious educators.

The concept of congregations as multigenerational, multicultural, educating communities working for social justice is in the ascendant today. This has implications for the use of appropriate, engaging methods in the programs we plan for ourselves and for our children, now and in the future.

Chapter Two

Nurturing the Spirit

"Like every other aspect of human potential, spiritual
development and growth is part of our birthright."
—Lisa Miller

Babies who are cared for—fed, comforted, kept warm and dry,
smiled at, spoken to gently, held in the arms of a loving person—
develop a sense of trust, the foundation of all faith. It is incumbent
on congregations to provide safe, comfortable nursery care for the
youngest who are entrusted to us by their parents. The need to feel
safe continues throughout our lifetimes and should always be a
consideration in planning programs and activities.

The developing infant expresses wonder and delight when
confronted with many new experiences. This sense of wonder and
awe continues and is especially acute in toddlers and preschoolers.
"A child's world is fresh, and new, and beautiful, full of wonder and
excitement," writes Rachel Carson.[37] Experiences with the natural
world help to keep this sense of wonder alive. Where outdoor
adventures aren't feasible, bring the natural world indoors with living
plants, shells, stones, flowers, twigs, leaves, bark, and (although it's
messy) with sand and water. Carson says that exploring nature with

17

a child is "largely a matter of becoming receptive to what lies all around you. It is learning again to use your eyes, ears, nostrils and finger tips, opening up the disused channels of sensory impression."[38]

The first spiritual experience I recall occurred on a crisp, clear night, when returning home from my grandmother's house after a day spent with our large extended family. I know that I was not yet five years old. My father carried me, my mother carried my little sister, and my older siblings walked ahead. My father said "Look!" and pointed to the starry sky. I still recall my feeling of connection with the earth on which my father stood, the sky above, and my family around me. Although the memory of this profound event has stayed with me for many years, it did not seem at all unusual at the time.

Children's Experiences

I am far from the only one to report such childhood experiences. The Religious Experience Research Unit at Manchester College, Oxford, gathered recollections from adults of childhood experiences of a transcendent nature. Edward Robinson's book *The Original Vision* is a study of the religious experience of children based on these accounts and his own observations. Robinson writes "It was with considerable excitement that on joining this research project I found myself reading this kind of thing: 'The most profound experience of my life came to me when I was very young, between 4 and 5 years old.' 'I just know that the whole of my life has been built on the great truth that was revealed to me then' (at the age of 6). 'As far back as I can remember I have never had a sense of separation from the spiritual force I now choose to call God.'"[39]

In *The Gift of Faith* Jeanne Nieuwejaar says "My spiritual life as a child was … organic, experienced not as something distinct and separate, but integrated in all phases of my living."[40] Even when adults do not report such recollections it is probably safe to assume that many, if not most, children have such experiences. A preschool child happily walking along was heard to sing with joy, over and over, "I am I. I am I." A six year old commented, "I really love my life." Another little girl, hugging herself, said to her mother, "I just love feeling my soul, don't you?"[41] Questions about birth and death and "Who made the world?" and "Why is it hard to be good?" show the reflective, spiritual character of the young child's life. An older child expressed his concerns about what existed before the Big Bang, the meaning of time, and who created God—all in about fifteen minutes. We do not need to teach children how to wonder (or worship), but to help them keep the sense of wonder they come equipped with.

In her 2015 book *The Spiritual Child*, clinical psychologist Lisa Miller reports on scientific research that suggests that "an 'inner spiritual compass' is an innate, concrete faculty … and a part of our biological endowment."[42] She defines spirituality as "an inner sense of living relationship to a higher power (God, nature, spirit, universe, the creator, or whatever your word is for the ultimate loving, guiding life-force)."[43] I differ slightly with her definition in that I would say a "deep connection with" the ultimate, and not necessarily experienced as "loving."

As we plan programs, what kind of experiences might we offer to support and nurture the spiritual aspects of development in children, youth, and adults? What learning activities are consistent with the goals of touching inward springs, stirring up the minds of learners, and inspiring a fervent love of truth?[44] What kind of experiences will evoke a sense of awe and reverence?

For children as much as possible these experiences should engage the body and the senses, through movement, touch, sound, and smell. Teaching should involve listening more than telling, engaging in exploration together more than instructing, and enjoying one another more than being an aloof presence. Activities that nurture a sense of responsibility, such as cleaning up after oneself and providing help to others as needed, are important. Providing resources for eager learners is more effective than any amount of lecturing.

Youth and Adults

Teens may be the most difficult age to plan for, but engaging them in the planning and providing resources usually works well. Youth generally like retreats, overnights, and outdoor events. They should have opportunities to experience the "highs" they need through worship and activities that evoke what is significant in life. Music, poetry, meditative practices, lighting candles, and singing are good activities for this. One teenager who did not regularly participate in religious education groups or church worship services found a real "high" at a General Assembly, when the rained-out outdoor service was held in a hotel ballroom. Bagpipers had been engaged to lead a procession from the hotel to the art museum for the service. Instead they brought the music into the ballroom. They played and played, marching around the ballroom, up and down stairs, and around the mezzanine. When they finished, this teen breathed into the silence "Now I know what it was like to be at Woodstock." I am aware that not everyone likes bagpipes. And one might hope for such lifting of spirit to occur without reference to Woodstock, but this experience opened the young teen to experience the whole of the worship service.

Many youth like to plan worship experiences for each other and for the congregation. Learning to do this well can be a valuable experience.

Adults do not come to classes and groups in churches for the specific learning needs they might take to the community college or the adult school. Rather, they come in search of learning that enhances their lives in a significant way. As formation is the goal of religious education for the young, so may transformation be the goal for adults.

The Fourth Level of Teaching

Opportunities arise in classroom or group situations for consideration of ultimate questions posed for the understanding of each age group. These are occasions when faith development or "religion making" may occur. In the late 1960s and early 1970s, values teaching came into its own, with "three levels of teaching" described by Simon and Harmin in an article in *Educational Leadership*. They lament that so much of teaching is at the "facts-for-facts level" and go on to say "There is a second level, a higher level, engagingly presented by Bruner, and this is called the concept level. We believe there is still a higher level, a level which makes use of facts and concepts, but which goes well beyond them in the direction of penetrating a student's life. This we call the values level."[45]

In religion making materials published by the UUA Eugene Navias adds a fourth level, celebration, to these three levels of teaching: fact, concept, and values. "We may consider, lift up, dedicate ourselves anew to values we hold in common.... We need to explore the possibilities for worshiping.... The biggest question for me as I think of planning programs every Sunday is 'how do I reach the level of valuing or personal meaning every time?'... Each session needs to invite children to look for meanings, personal applications, and thus be 'religion making.'"[46]

Planning a structure that encourages participation at this fourth level is important. Perhaps the easiest way to do this is through a brief closure at the end of each session, when children and leaders may wish to share responses to the morning's experience. This time may include sitting in a circle, a familiar song or saying, and the lighting of a candle or chalice. It may enrich individuals' lives while serving to build community, through ritual and shared celebration.

The Importance of Ritual

Ritual is an intentional process, designed to evoke appropriate responses for the occasion. Bedtime rituals—a story, hugs, tucking in, quiet conversation about the day, perhaps a bedtime prayer—encourage quiet, comfort, and sleep. Mealtime rituals—holding hands, saying grace, even the simple act of quietly unfolding napkins and placing them in laps, create community and settle bodily systems for nourishment. Rituals in faith development programs should evoke the sense of wonder, a feeling of community, and an openness to consider things of worth.

Children learn family culture through ritual in the home and family; children and adults learn, and re-learn, their faith and practice through ritual in the religious community.[47] As they are involved in the creation or adaptation of family rituals, so too may they help to create or adapt the rituals in the religious education classroom. Children may take turns saying a few words at chalice lighting time, or (with adult help for the youngest) light the chalice. The teacher can see that each child has an opportunity to share in the ritual opening or closing, always leaving the right to pass as an option.

Such moments may occur spontaneously. One of the most meaningful "communion services" I have ever experienced was such an event. Many years ago, so long ago that the story I was reading was about Martin and Judy "in their two little houses," I substituted in a kindergarten class. At the end of a warm and comfortable morning, Roy quietly moved away from the group and began preparing "pretend" coffee in the housekeeping corner. Amy, observing this movement, joined him. Neither spoke, and the others continued to focus on the story. As the story ended, the two poured and served cups for everyone and passed around a tray of invisible treats. There was a long companionable silence as we shared this experience.

In a book primarily for Montessori teachers but applicable for others as well, Aline Wolf talks about nurturing the spirit of the child in non-sectarian classrooms. She distinguishes between spirituality and religion this way: "Spirituality is a basic quality of human nature; the practice of a particular religion is the way that many people choose to give voice to their spirituality."[48] Much of what she has to say applies to religious education classrooms as well. One example is the need to provide a space and time for silence. Certainly young children cannot be expected to maintain silence for long periods of time, but it is not difficult to establish a practice of being quiet and still for brief moments. Special spaces and times set aside for quiet, says Wolf, allow "one to be open to one's inner voice."[49] This is true for adults as well as children of all ages.

The child's sense of wonder is aroused by observations of nature in its many manifestations but also in the classroom with activities planned for that purpose. These may involve light and color, cycles of nature, care of the earth, the dark, shadow play, rainbows created by prisms, care of pets, growing plants in the classroom and perhaps out of doors, and nature walks at every season.

Art and music—observational or participatory—help the child to get in touch with inner peace, goodness, the joy and sadness of living, as experienced in the community of faith. Times of meditation, group reflection on shared experiences, and respectful attentiveness to one another have the same effect.

Children and God Talk

Whether parents are humanist, atheist, agnostic, pagan, theist, Christian, earth centered, or "none of the above," children will almost certainly speak of God. And perhaps more of a concern for the teacher, *ask* about God. Wolf's suggestions for dealing with conversations and questions about God may be helpful to volunteer teachers. "We should not be surprised when children talk about God. It is a word that is in most children's vocabulary—a word they have heard at home as well as in places of worship. And it is a word that undoubtedly will enter our … classrooms. How should we handle it? With respect, with understanding, with honesty."[50] Even when a child's expressed thought about God seems ludicrous to adults, it should be treated with respect. The same may be said for prayer. One little boy familiar with prayer at home, found it accessible when the family experienced car trouble on a little-traveled road on a dark night. His immediate response was to say "Dear God, please turn on the moon." Children who hear adults use the word God as an all-purpose kind of expression, such as "Oh, my God!" will likely use it that way as well.

While teachers may feel uncomfortable with questions that touch on the transcendent, Wolf suggests that such questions should be honored as audible signs of a child's developing spirituality and that "I have often wondered about that myself" is an honest, respectful answer.[51] Listening carefully to children's comments and questions about God, or any form of transcendence, the teacher may be able to frame responses and questions for the child appropriately. When saying what we think, we should be careful to frame it as our belief or opinion, not as a definitive answer about things no one can answer with certainty. In other words, "I believe such and such, but others think so and so … " This may lead to a child's own statement of belief, and "What do you think?" is a legitimate question to ask.

Bushnell saw children as becoming Christian through a lifelong process of living in a Christian family and in a Christian church; whatever the theology of the family or congregation, we may assume that faith development occurs in such a way. Channing saw the home as a primary influence, as well. When home and congregation share common goals and each supplements the other's work, the child benefits. Parents often come to our congregations seeking enrichment and expansion of what they do at home to help their children develop a life of faith. In addition to programs and classes, living in religious community offers other opportunities for faith development. Attending worship services and community events, participating in social justice work with others, and finding models for faithful living play a significant role in faith development.

Richard Gilbert suggests that four key religious developmental tasks for the child, "a richness of deep experiences for subsequent reflection—a basic trust in life/faith in existence—a sense of personal worthwhileness—a reverence for life beyond the self," are integral to one another.[52] These are tasks to be addressed through our programs.

When we re-frame religious education as "religious growth and learning" or "teaching and learning for faith development," we are more likely to "minister to the religious life of the child." Searle notes that it is not necessary to "discourse at length about the religious experience of children," but that it is a "mystery to be respected." He notes some of the "symptoms" of their experience of that mystery: the sense of engagement, quiet joy, and "short, sharp insights offered spontaneously by children that, together with their drawings, represent the fruits of their contemplation of the mystery."[53]

Programs that help to keep the mystery and wonder of the young child alive, and to help others to reclaim it, are vital to faith formation.

Chapter Three

How We Learn: Theory

"A good theory is one that holds together long enough
to get you to a better theory." —Donald O. Hebb

That people can and do learn is indisputable; what they are doing
when they learn and how they do it is in question. There are many
theories but no real agreement about the complex process of learning.
How people learn remains something of a mystery. Psychologists,
philosophers, neurophysiologists, educators, and social scientists
have tackled the subject. Parents and teachers alike have both exulted
and despaired over it.

A quick review of the literature will confirm the lack of
agreement. Some lists, in books and online, call the same theory by
different names or combine two or more; some categorize individual
proponents in different ways. One website lists five paradigms of
learning theory: behaviorism, cognitivism, constructivism, design-
based, and humanism, with a number of different theories within
each of these paradigms. In addition this website defines descriptive,
meta, and identity theories. It lists two miscellaneous learning
theories and models: affordance theory and multiple intelligences.[54]
Another site examines twelve different theories: constructivism,

behaviorism, Piaget's developmental theory, neuroscience, brain-based learning, learning styles, multiple intelligences, right brain/left brain thinking, communities of practice, control theory, observational learning, and social cognition.[55]

Theories evolve and change as theorists continue their study and evaluate experiences, and the different theories inform one another. Certainly, research informs practice, but practice leads to additional research and thus informs theory.

There *is* general agreement that change occurs when learning takes place: a new skill may be acquired, knowledge may be attained, deeper understanding may emerge. Peter Jarvis says that learning is "the driving force through which the human essence emerges and is nurtured."[56] He examined four primary learning theories—behaviorism, cognitive, emotive, and experiential—in an effort to see if it is possible to develop a comprehensive theory of learning, and concluded that although this was not possible, "Each of our theories of learning adds a little bit more to our understanding of human life and learning, but we do not and cannot know everything about it."[57]

Learning different types of things requires different ways of learning. Skills such as riding a bike or swimming are learned primarily by doing, although observations and instruction play a part. Mastering a body of knowledge, or learning specific information, may involve books, the internet, lectures, discussion, and other methods. Life learnings about relationships, work, success and failure, grief and loss, are more complicated. However, individuals have their own ways of learning. The main thing we need to know as religious leaders who teach and help others to teach, is that people learn in a variety of ways and that we will therefore do well to teach in a variety of ways.

Unitarian Universalist religious education learning theory has been informed primarily by the views of John Dewey (learning by doing, problem solving, project, experience reflected on), Jerome Bruner (process of education and the spiral curriculum) and more recently Maria Montessori (Godly Play and Spirit Play) and Howard

Gardner (Multiple Intelligences). Most teachers seem to draw on more than one specific learning theory as they experience success (or failure) in their teaching.

Danish educator Knud Illeris put together a collection of essays, written since 1990, by internationally known learning theorists. The book provides a fairly detailed synthesis of current learning theories. Illeris says "we have today a picture of a great variety of learning theoretical approaches and constructions, which are more-or-less compatible and more-or-less competitive on the global academic market."[58] Illeris writes about four kinds of learning: cumulative or mechanical, assimilative (learning by addition), accommodation or transcendent (which both relinquishes and reconstructs) and transformative (previously called significant, expansive, or transitional by others). Jack Mezirow, who came up with the term transformative, has a chapter in the book. In connection with adult learning, much attention has been given of late to this theory.[59]

The influence of Dewey is present in several of the chapters, most specifically in Bente Elkjaer's essay on pragmatism. Elkjaer writes about Dewey's "notion of experience based on transaction between subject and worlds as well as in the relation between action and thinking" and suggests "practice" as a better term for what Dewey was discussing.[60] David Kolb's experiential learning is discussed in Jarvis' chapter on "learning to be a person in society" and elsewhere in the book.[61] Bruner is represented with a chapter on "Culture, Mind and Education."[62] Gardner writes about entry points, telling analogies, and approaching the core, all from the vantage point of multiple intelligences.[63]

Developmental Theory

Learning theory is closely related to theories of human development. These abound and extend to faith development. Most readers are likely to be familiar with some: Piagetan, Psycho-Social (Eric Erickson), Moral (Lawrence Kolberg and Carol Gilligan), and

Faith Development (James Fowler). Gabriel Moran has proposed "religious education development" as a better way to look at what we are doing in the work of faith development. He posits three religious states, each with two "moments."

The first is Simply Religious, lasting from birth to the age of five or seven. The two moments in this stage are The Physical and The Mythic. He says that "this period of life simply manifests two connected characteristics that apply to life as a whole." These, he suggests, are that whatever good comes to the child is a gift, and that the child is part of a community.[64] In the first Moment, "the religious life of the small child is one of unending mystery and unalloyed wonder. The divine is everywhere, manifested in life's daily miracles." In the second Moment, he says, "the divine is a power manifest in all intense experiences" and it is a time of "brilliant imagery and powerful stories."[65]

The second stage, that of Acquiring a Religion, is composed of two Moments: that of learning the belief of "our people" and then questioning, or "disbelieving." This period covers the time period from the age of five or six well into adolescence.[66] The third Stage Moran calls "Religiously Christian (Jewish, Muslim, etc.)" and we might call "Religiously Unitarian Universalist." Moran has named the first Moment in this stage "Parable," noting that persons "pass beyond the negative stance of disbelief and decide to set their hearts on something." He explains that parables make us "reflect on life's paradoxes and inequities" so we move forward with a parabolic attitude. In the second Moment of this stage the parabolic attitude is "deepened and enriched by the development of a contemplative center to life."[67]

Multiple Intelligences

For the religious educator, Gardner's theory of multiple intelligences offers a framework for designing learning experiences that will meet the needs of a wide variety of learners. This theory confirms something educators have known for a long time, that people learn in different ways, and tells us how and why that is so. He uses eight criteria—drawn from biological sciences, logical analysis, developmental psychology, and traditional psychological research—to determine the intelligences. The criteria are: isolation as a brain function, evolutionary history and plausibility, susceptibility to encoding in a symbol system, identifiable set of core operations, distinct developmental history, the existence of idiot savants and prodigies, support from experimental psychological tasks, and support from psychometric research.[68]

Since he presented this theory in *Frames of Mind* in 1983, many have adapted and enlarged upon it. The eight intelligences identified by Gardner and expanded by others are:

1. Linguistic (sometimes called verbal-linguistic)
2. Logical-mathematical
3. Visual-spatial
4. Bodily-kinesthtetic
5. Musical (sometimes called musical-rhythmic)
6. Interpersonal
7. Intrapersonal
8. Naturalist

The first seven were present in *Frames of Mind;* he added naturalist later.[69]

A ninth intelligence has been suggested: existential or spiritual. The two terms have been used interchangeably, but Gardner makes a distinction between the two. In his book *Intelligence Reframed*: "I conclude that the narrowly defined variety of spiritual intelligence here termed 'existential' may well be admissible, while the more broadly defined 'spiritual intelligence' is not." Two pages later he writes, "Despite the attractiveness of a ninth intelligence, however, I am not adding existential intelligence to the list. I find the phenomenon perplexing enough and the distance from the other intelligences vast enough to dictate prudence—at least for now. At most I am willing, Fellini-style, to joke about '8 ½ intelligences.'"[70]

Carolyn Chapman has come up with an engaging format identifying a shoe for each of the intelligences as a catchy guide to understanding them:

1. The tap shoe, the "communicating shoe," for verbal-linguistic
2. The hiking boot, with its pattern of laces, for logical-mathematical
3. Cinderella's glass slipper, representing "imagination and creativity" for the visual-spatial intelligence
4. The athletic shoe (obviously) for bodily-kinesthetic
5. The drum major's boot, "keeping the band in rhythm as it plays" for the musical-rhythmic
6. The football cleat, representing teamwork, for the interpersonal
7. The comfortable bedroom slipper for the intrapersonal
8. The Native American moccasin for the naturalist intelligence[71]

Participants at the Renaissance Program's Teacher Support and Training Module in the Pacific Southwest District were asked: "What shoe might represent the existential/spiritual intelligence?" Several replied instantly: "Barefooted!"

The religious education leader seeking to utilize an understanding of multiple intelligences will find many possible applications. For the linguistic or "word smart" learner, listening, conversation, storytelling, creative writing, and reading are good approaches to any topic. The logical-mathematical learner is said to be number or logic smart and will appreciate activities using patterns and sequences, puzzles, technology and gadgets. Drawing, painting, working with clay, making collages, sewing, and using all types of media appeal to the visual-spatial or "art smart" learner.

Dancing and other movement activities, the use of manipulatives, tactile experiences, and construction projects using large muscles appeal to the bodily-kinesthetic or "body smart" learner. The musical-rhythmic or "sound smart" learner responds to the use of musical instruments, singing, listening to music.

The "people smart" or interpersonal learner does well in group projects, such as painting murals, planning presentations, conversation, and any activity involving interaction with others, while the intrapersonal or "self smart" learner likes to have time for quiet reflection or journaling. Observing and interacting with nature is important to the naturalist or "nature smart" learner. In a classroom this may involve care of plants and small animals, but outdoor field trips provide opportunities for hands-on learning.

Practical Applications

Thomas Armstrong suggests many learning activities for each of the intelligences in a book intended for full-day secular schools. While not all of the activities are suitable for (nor would fit in) the format for religious education programming, they may suggest other activities for such programs. His idea for eight activity centers, or tables, each with a board game appealing to a particular intelligence, would be good for a multigenerational game night in a congregation.[72] Armstrong says "the theory of multiple intelligences has broad implications for special education," suggesting that educators focus on strengths of special needs students, rather than deficits.[73]

The "entry points" Gardner suggests in his chapter are narrative, quantitative-numerical, foundational/existential, aesthetic, hands-on and social. "An 'entry point' perspective," he writes, "places students directly in the center of a disciplinary topic, arousing their interests and securing cognitive commitment for further exploration."[74]

Most people learn in more than one way, and their "preferred learning style" as well as their most developed intelligence may be among many ways they like to learn. While studies have not shown that learners actually learn better using their strongest or preferred Intelligence, it makes sense to offer options that make learning more interesting and fun. In religious education groups, where goals include community building and helping each person to feel comfortable, the effort to provide learning experiences that are suited to each participant is especially important. There are probably occasions, however, when we might well want to challenge learners by helping them to expand their ways of knowing. According to Bruce Joyce, "To help students grow, we need to generate what we currently term a *dynamic disequilibrium*. Rather than matching teaching approaches to students in such a way as to minimize discomfort, our task is to expose the students to new teaching modalities that will, for some time, be uncomfortable to them."[75] Gardner himself cautions against trying to teach any subject through too many ways of learning. He says that using a scattershot approach for each topic is a waste of effort and time. "But, *any* uniform educational approach is likely to serve only a few children optimally."[76]

Whatever theories teachers subscribe to, many variables affect learning in the classroom. This means we have to consider practice as well as theory when planning.

Chapter Four

How We Learn: Issues in Practice

"The proof is in the pudding."
—Old Saying

Taking theory into the classroom is all very well, but in practice many issues and concerns may affect the complex process of learning. In my experience volunteer teachers often take more seriously things that go awry during class time and less seriously the need to plan for the best learning environment possible. Those who plan carefully ahead of time usually have more enjoyable and fulfilling experiences as teachers.

Preparation—of the room, teaching materials, and the teaching team—is an important part of the educational process. Learning is enhanced when the room, the teachers, and the learners are prepared. Many discipline issues (if not most) can be avoided by adequate advance preparation for the session. The importance of preparing the environment cannot be overstated. Many congregations expect teachers to come in early enough to set up whatever is needed, but to the extent possible, paid staff or non-teaching volunteers should prepare the rooms ahead of time and have requested materials at the ready.

Preparation

The learning environment is critical to the learning experience. Learners thrive in an appropriate environment, struggle in one that is not suitable. Physical and emotional space influence not only the behavior and attentiveness of learners, but also their learning. Ideally, each classroom would be set up for: the size of the class, the age and general developmental level of those in the group, and planned activities. In practice, this is rarely the case. Most rooms are used by different groups, often rented to a preschool with its attendant rich environment of toys, games, manipulatives, and so on. In some cases there is an expectation that these things will not be touched by the congregation's Sunday morning participants. Rental agreements that are specific about room use and arrangements provide a non-confrontational way to assure that the room is suitable for the program. Topics to cover in such an agreement include: what will be left in the room, how off-limits equipment and materials will be removed, turned around so that a display place is available, or covered in an attractive way. Unless it is Halloween, furnishings should not be draped with white cloths. A room with bare walls is preferable to one where walls are covered by unrelated posters, drawings, and the like. The room may then be set up with a few simple things appropriate for the religious education class.

When Parker Palmer speaks of the importance of getting ready, he is talking about something more than setting up the chairs and putting out the paints. I agree with his comment that preparation "of a learning space" requires competence, time, and energy, at least as much "as preparing a good lecture—and more than preparing a bad one."[77] He uses the word "space" to mean "a complex of factors: the physical arrangement and feeling of the room, the conceptual framework that I build around the topic my students and I are exploring, the emotional ethos I hope to facilitate, and the ground rules that will guide our inquiry."[78]

It is important for the teacher to be familiar with the content to be explored during class time and to have necessary resources available so as not to disrupt the flow of activities. Recruitment of teachers should include forthright statements of expectations and the amount of time that may be involved in preparation. In addition to studying the content and preparing activities and materials, another aspect of preparation is to open oneself to the experience and to be emotionally and spiritually ready. Curriculum materials have often offered inspirational readings for the teacher to prepare for planning and leading each session. The UUA's Tapestry of Faith offers suggestions for spiritual preparation of teachers in every workshop, and a recorded PowerPoint of a webinar on the subject is online. For some teachers, just knowing that methods and materials have been prepared and taking a few deep breaths may be all that is needed for centering the self. When possible, I like to have quiet music playing as I finish preparations and welcome the group.

Students can also be prepared for appropriate attention to classroom activities. When children come one at a time, the teacher or a helper may introduce a quiet activity or engage in quiet conversation with the children, rather than leaving one or more to mill about aimlessly. When they come in a group—as they do when coming from the worship service—it helps if they are brought in an orderly (but not rigid) fashion by a teacher or helper and encouraged to be seated in a circle. This is where the doorkeeper concept from Godly Play and Spirit Play may be especially helpful. An assistant may serve this function, allowing the teacher to be seated to welcome all into the circle. This should be done even if the first activity is planned as a time for options, in order to create an appropriate mood for the morning. After children are greeted and attendance is noted, planned activities may then begin.

If adults in the classroom are calm, focused, and attentive to the children and the functioning of the group, it helps learners to be as well. Teachers and helpers should limit their conversations to what is pertinent to their teaching in the moment. Parents (and other adults) should move their conversations elsewhere. At the end of class time, parents should respect the closing activity and not interrupt. Early or late pickups are disruptive to the planned learning process. For teen and adult classes, a ritual opening may be all that is needed to set the stage for learning.

Most children are good at gauging what is expected of them, so it behooves the teacher to expect appropriate behavior. Religious bodies seeking more diversity must adapt to a variety of cultural and familial norms, but some order is essential and adults may set behavioral expectations. Classes are often encouraged to adopt their own rules, but these must align with congregational policies and teacher expectations. The practice of establishing behavioral covenants often ignores such constraints, but even if every child suggests a rule that involves serving ice cream every Sunday, that is certainly not realistic in practice. When such covenants are established, it is best to extend the process over several weeks to insure involvement of most of the group.

Developmental Issues and Behavioral Concerns

Most curriculum materials will have information about typical developmental characteristics for the age group for which the materials are intended. Tracey Hurd's book *Nurturing Children and Youth* is a developmental guidebook that will help teachers learn more about the age groups they are teaching. "Each person has an individual, evolving path of growth and development," says Hurd, although there are some more or less typical characteristics at different ages. The key areas of development discussed in Hurd's book are: cognitive, social, emotional, moral, and spiritual.[79]

There are sure to be variations in developmental levels—physical, in addition to those above—even in a closely graded group. These need to be taken into account when planning learning activities. A structured environment is especially helpful for children with disabilities. All children may benefit from a structure that allows for some flexibility. When two adults are always in the room, one may work with the one or two children who are less (or more) advanced than the others, or who have difficulties fitting into the group. When optional activities are available for part of the session, children can self-select if there are activities of varying difficulty.

Every child—every person—should feel welcome in the group and great care must be taken to assure that for those with special needs. A general policy for inclusion should be in place, with the understanding that each person's needs are different. Parental involvement in planning for the child with special needs is essential. Such a plan for each child with special needs may include the use of helpers (peers or adult volunteers), appropriate arrangement of spaces for wheelchairs or crutches, and agreements for managing behavior. Sally Patton has suggested that the structure of Spirit Play "works well for some special needs children."[80] and that "most overly active children respond well to this environment."[81] Placement in mixed-age or multigenerational groupings is helpful also. Thomas Armstrong suggests ways in which attention to Multiple Intelligences is useful for children with special needs.[82] He says that by focusing on growth paradigms rather than deficits "MI theory thus provides a model for understanding the autistic savant who cannot communicate clearly with others but plays music at a professional level, the dyslexic who possesses special drawing or designing gifts, the 'developmentally disabled' student who can act extremely well on the stage, or the student with cerebral palsy who has special linguistic and logical genius.'"[83]

Some children have difficulty meeting *any* behavioral norm expectations. These may include children who take medication throughout the week but not on Sundays and have a hard time focusing, children who are brought against their will and may understandably feel uncooperative, and children who frequently say, "I'm bored." They can be encouraged to do something that interests them, when options are available. These options might include books, puzzles, simple activity centers. Many children will be bored if lectured, read to in a monotone, or badgered about sitting still.

Positive encouragement is preferred over harsh or punitive comments. Say something like "Hands in front of us, everyone." "Each person on his or her own mat" is better than "No touching" or "Keep your hands off others." A general statement that doesn't call attention to any one person is often better than speaking directly to one child. After all, sometimes attention may be the goal of the behavior. Gentle touching on the shoulder may calm or quiet some children. It is best if all are in the circle for at least the primary lesson portion of the morning, but some children may only listen attentively if allowed to quietly work with clay, handle manipulatives, or water plants, in another part of the room.

While a relaxed, open attitude toward behavior may be desirable, there are variations in the expectations of individual teachers and in their ability to deal with behavioral issues. Teachers learn about their students through observation and their own understandings of what works, a good argument for a consistent adult presence. A teaching team of three persons might work like this: one week A is lead teacher and B helper; the next week B is teacher and C helper, and the next C is teacher and A helper (although it need not be so rigidly organized). All might be present on some few occasions, even in a small class. If there are four on the team, for the sake of continuity, it is not advisable to divide into two teams who teach together on a rotating basis.

In my experience, a child who will not recognize limits and behave appropriately after redirection, should not be allowed to remain in the classroom. Of course this should not be the first reaction when a child is uncooperative! Even if necessary only the primary or head teacher should make the decision to remove a child, not a one-time volunteer or anyone unfamiliar with the situation and the child. Removal should be a last resort, not a first thought. Berryman thinks a child should be removed from the room, or restrained, only "if the safety of the children is threatened by a child who is out of control." He does, however, ask a disruptive child to move from the circle to sit with the doorkeeper. This works only if there is a doorkeeper, of course.[84]

For removal to work, there has to be somewhere for the child to go, and the atmosphere should not be punitive, but perhaps a little boring. Not being allowed to remain in the class and disrupt it is a natural (and logical) consequence of lack of cooperation with the situation. The child should not be left alone, but have an adult nearby.

In one small congregation with few children some of those few were accustomed to being uncooperative (and at times quite disruptive) during the religious education hour. After meetings with parents, professional staff, and teachers, it was agreed that one of the teachers would take the disruptive child to a parent in the service. In the event that the child refused to leave, one teacher would go to get the parent to come for the child. Once the children realized that this plan was a reality, there was no occasion to use it. In an ideal situation there would have been someone other than one of the teachers available to do this. If there are enough volunteers available to provide adult supervision, a quiet room where those who can't maintain decorum in the classroom can choose from quiet activities until ready to return to the classroom works well. Sometimes the religious educator's office is a good option for a separate space, but there too the atmosphere should not be punitive.

Many volunteer teachers are reluctant to cooperate with such a plan, perhaps feeling that it reflects poorly on their teaching skills. It should be explained to them that enabling a child's inappropriate behavior is a mistake for the child's social development.

Diversity and Inclusivity

In practice, we should keep in mind our overall goal of inclusivity. Diversity in the classroom is to be desired. In teaching for diversity, consistent use of language, pictures, stories, and songs featuring a variety of people will go a long way toward making a diverse population not only seem normal but to be expected. Curriculum materials should illustrate racial, ethnic, identity, ability, and class diversity to encourage optimum inclusivity.

The LREDA Integrity Team has developed materials to help those who plan and carry out religious education programs evaluate curricula, welcome and represent diversity, and be sensitive to cultural representation. These materials may be found on the organization's website.[85]

Teachers are often advised to have more material than they think they can use during a class period in case it is needed. That said, care must be taken not to try to teach *too much* in limited class time. Howard Gardner maintains that issues arise when we try to cover too much material. "As long as you are determined to cover everything, you actually ensure that most kids are not going to understand. You've got to take enough time to get kids deeply involved in something so that they can think about it in lots of different ways and apply it."[86]

It is a good idea to have more activities planned than you think you will need, but also a good idea to allow lots of time to explore each point as long as there is interest, rather than doing everything planned. Presenting and elaborating on one idea in depth may be more valuable than a broad approach that barely touches the surface. Exploring one story through a variety of experiences, as in Rotation, is a good example of this. Another is having learning centers that can be visited over and over again.

Social justice is rightfully an emphasis in religious education. Caring for others is significant in faith development. But social justice should begin in the classroom. Name calling, teasing, bullying, hitting, or any other form of discrimination should not be permitted at any age. Just as teachers should show respect for learners, so too should learners treat teachers with respect. This is an aspect of planning for activities, also. By school age, many children enjoy reading and writing and may have opportunities to do so in our programs, as optional activities, but it is unjust to require such work of children who struggle with these all week in school settings.

At the end of the session, time should be allowed for participants to clean up. If materials are mishandled during class time, remove them and say "You can work with this next time." Offer an alternative activity. It is no service to children to allow them to create messes for others to deal with. Teachers may help children to be responsible for their own appropriate behavior and encourage them toward self-discipline. Helpful books and training programs are those for Training for Effective Teaching (T.E.T.) based on the work of Thomas Gordon, and Systematic Training for Effective Teaching (S.T.E.T) based on the work of Rudolf Dreikurs, Don Dinkmeyer and Gary McKay.

Whatever our theories about learning, circumstances need to be taken into account. Even when the environment, teachers, and learners are prepared and engaging activities are planned, things may not go as well as hoped. Good teaching is often problem solving; the teachers should ask each other "What can we do better next time?"

Chapter Five

How We Teach: Approaches

"To teach is to show someone how to live."
—Gabriel Moran

What we know (or believe) about how people learn will influence how we teach, but so too will our approach to teaching—our pedagogy. The values and principles of the religious community play an important role as well. Teaching approaches considered in this chapter include text-centered, teacher-centered, child-centered, subject-centered, shared praxis, showing how, teaching as spiritual guidance, discovery/inquiry, and teaching for understanding, as well as Montessori.

Some of these approaches are more consistent with liberal values and principles than others. Text-centered, for example, is the least consistent with them, at least for most children most of the time. Aspects of some are compatible with others, but some (such as teacher-centered and student-centered) stand in opposition to one another. It was in response to this polarity that Parker Palmer suggested "subject-centered" as an approach.

The Text-centered or Teacher-centered Classroom

The use of "schooling" to describe a certain type of education came into usage during the 1960s. In the schooling model of education, text and teacher are authorities and experts, there to impart fixed and certain knowledge to students. Educational theorist Paulo Freire called this concept of education the "banking system," where students are seen as empty bank accounts and teachers deposit funds—information—into them, resulting in passive learning.[87] Many have experienced such teaching, and for some it is the only way they know to teach. There may be occasions where an acknowledged expert or authority on a subject may be the teacher, when it is appropriate to be teacher-centered. This is the case in a lecture series or an adult forum.

The catechism is an old and familiar form of text-centered education. Eugene Navias wrote about the catechism in a syllabus for graduate students in religious education:

> From the mainstreams of Protestantism which they had left, both Unitarians and Universalists took the catechism as the method of imparting their truths.... "A Catechism for the Use of Children" by The Reverend William Bourne Oliver Peabody, written in 1823 for the instruction of children at the First Unitarian Church of Springfield, MA, became widely known in Unitarian circles and was revised and republished in 1849. Uniquely as catechisms go, it was written in verse and was intended to be sung.[88]

Although the catechism began to lose favor, the materials developed and used throughout the nineteenth and early twentieth centuries by both Unitarians and Universalists featured Bible-centered lessons and were didactic in style and substance.[89] Even today there are occasions, especially when teaching factual material, that the question and answer method may be used. Some children especially enjoy rote learning and memorization, at least in small doses and when done with a spirit of fun. They appreciate being able to recite the Seven Principles or a congregation's covenant on their own.

In one congregation where children were in congregational worship only three times each year, the religious education committee asked teachers to have children in their classes memorize the covenant beginning "Love is the teaching of this church" that adults used in the service each week. Most teachers were reluctant and most children resistant, so that was not a successful effort. Later children were included in the first part of the service every Sunday. They quickly learned the covenant! Attending the service regularly and saying the covenant with others in the congregation gave meaning to the words. One of those children visited a different congregation as a college student and, noting its different style of worship than what she was used to, expressed doubt that it was a "real" Unitarian Universalist church. She reported with indignation that "They didn't even say, 'Love is the teaching of this church.'"

Child-centered Education

In 1893 the *Annual Report of the Board of Directors* to the Sunday School Society noted that president Edward A. Horton had urged churches to adopt more progressive methods of education, to abandon catechisms, and to base their work on a greater trust in the child, with the aim of developing reliance on an inner, rather than an outer, authority. The Unitarian curriculum series published in 1912 reflected this new philosophy. "'Hitherto, lessons in religion have been largely material-centered. Our proposal is that these lessons shall be child-centered.'"[90]

Religious education grew from the same roots as American public education, with John Dewey and other Progressives as primary influences. This approach to teaching is characterized by experiential learning, child-centered curriculum, and an emphasis on the whole child. Dewey recognized as vital to education "what already existed in the child—interest in conversation, inquiry, construction, and artistic expression."[91] This has been the philosophy undergirding curriculum development and the primary mode of teaching recommended for religious education through the years and continues to challenge and inspire both secular and religious educators.

Best Practice teaching (a contemporary take on progressive, child-centered education) is presented by Harvey Daniels and Marilyn Bizar in their book *Methods That Matter*. They note that Progressive branches of school reform movements have always been guided and inspired by the work of John Dewey.[92] "Best Practice is a … term that points to the same basic set of overlapping beliefs and practices that has been struggling for acceptance in American schools for generations."[93] Four vital ingredients of Best Practice are: choice, responsibility, expression, and community.[94] This kind of teaching mirrors much of the best in teaching for religious growth and learning in classrooms.

A focus on the whole child is especially important with young children. It is important for the young child to feel at home, safe, and comfortable in the congregational setting; creating such an atmosphere is critical for early learning. While it may seem natural to shift from child-centered to subject-centered teaching as students mature, person-centered teaching for adults may be found in Small Group Ministry and some personal workshop learning opportunities, such as spirituality groups. We might call this approach learner-centered or student-centered.

Subject-centered Teaching

Parker Palmer notes that some educators are torn between "the teacher-centered model, with its concern for rigor and the student-centered model, with its concern for active learning." He proposes that the classroom should be neither teacher-centered nor student-centered but subject-centered. "Modeled on the community of truth, this is a classroom in which teacher and students alike are focused on a great thing, a classroom in which the best features of teacher- and student-centered education are merged and transcended."[95] He goes on to say, "When student and teacher are the only active agents, community easily slips into narcissism, where either the teacher reigns supreme or the students can do no wrong.... The subject-centered classroom is characterized by the fact that the third thing has a presence so real, so vivid, so vocal that it can hold teacher and students alike accountable for what they say and do."[96] He says that the learning "space should honor the 'little stories' of the individual and the 'big' stories of the disciplines and traditions." [97] "Individuals" applies to teachers and students alike.

This will often be the approach used in adult religious education, where people have chosen to study a particular topic.

Shared Praxis

Thomas Groome is chiefly responsible for introducing shared praxis, based on the work of Brazilian liberation educator Paulo Freire, to Unitarian Universalist religious educators. He has called shared praxis a teaching approach, rather than a theory or method. "In a definite sense," he writes, "I intend it to be both."[98] Shared praxis begins with a focusing activity and has the following movements:

1. Present Action (often called Naming our Knowing)
2. Critical Reflection on that Present Action, or Knowing
3. Presentation of Community Story and Vision
4. Dialectic between Community Story and Vision and personal story and vision
5. A faith response for the future[99]

The focusing activity is similar to Gardner's "entry points," discussed in Chapter Three.

Many teaching methods and learning activities may be used with the shared praxis approach: for example, the focusing activity may be a song, an object, a story, a picture or collage, or something else entirely. And a variety of methods may be used in the following movements.

Shared praxis has been used in curriculum development and lesson planning in Unitarian Universalist programs for many years. It is particularly well suited to a study of social justice issues. Students—older children, as well as adults—bring forward issues that concern them and the group, after reflection and consideration, makes a decision for social action.

Showing How

"Showing how" is Gabriel Moran's contribution to the teaching approach lexicon. He suggests that the first form of teaching is bodily and hands-on. He says, "I think that 'show how' is the best beginning phrase for describing teaching." When the child says "show me how" to swim, or to ride a bicycle, or to tie a shoe, that is the only method that will work. "Showing how," he says, "starts with bodily gestures that invite a bodily response."[100] Moran goes beyond the bodily, however, as is clear from his conclusion "To teach is to show someone how to live and die."[101]

Moran is concerned with language, and specifically what he calls the languages of teaching. "For teachers in religious education, the effect of a rationalistic meaning of teaching is to limit the possibilities of their work. Any effective teaching of a religious way of life requires a range of settings for teaching: in the family, in the religious congregation, in struggles for justice, in contemplative silence, as well as in the classroom."[102] This approach suggests the importance of the teacher as an exemplar.

Moran writes also about "teaching with the end in view" and "teaching when the end is not in view." He posits three forms of teaching when the end is in view: storytelling, lecturing, preaching a sermon."[103] When teaching in a religious setting, the end (developing faith-full persons) while worthy, may not be in view.

Teaching as Spiritual Guidance

Teaching Maori children in New Zealand, Sylvia Ashton-Warner found that those who could not read using the British textbooks and methods approved by the government, could not only read, but also write, books of their own, using the self-chosen words of the Key Vocabulary. These words—brought to the process by five year olds—were not bland, insipid "first reader" words, but rather words filled with power and meaning, and reflective of their own lives: kiss, frightened, kill, gun, ghost, beer, police, Granny, drunk. They sometimes suggested words that later proved not to be of critical interest; they couldn't recognize them on second sight. This never happened with "kiss" or with "frightened," an unusually hard word for new readers![104] She used music in the classroom, playing the piano or encouraging spontaneous singing or dancing, following sometimes the lead of the children.

Ashton-Warner's "organic teaching"[105] was profoundly religious, in that it helped children reach within themselves for what they wanted, and needed, to learn. The perception of Ashton-Warner's fictional counterpart in *Teacher* was that the program developed for the white population tended to repress the native culture, and was not effective for the Maori children. It was, I think, a good example of the teacher as a spiritual guide. She did not carry the children where someone else wanted them to go, but rather helped them equip themselves for their own journeys.

"It is the teacher who is at the heart of our programs," writes Roberta Nelson in an essay in *Essex Conversations*. She suggests that the teacher is a spiritual guide who affirms and challenges, questions and encourages.[106] This approach to teaching bears little resemblance to the schooling model approach of teacher as expert and authority. Among others who have written of teaching as spiritual guidance is

Barry Andrews. He says "what is important in religious education is not how much you know about children, teaching or even Unitarian Universalism, but how much you are willing to give of yourself, of your soul.... Above all, teachers are mentors and companions of the children as they undertake their religious journeys in life."[107]

Montessori

Montessori education is based on the work of Maria Montessori, a nineteenth-century Italian doctor who became known as an educator through the success of her tenement schools. Her approach required an orderly, structured environment and the use of manipulatives and other materials in prescribed ways.

Montessori's insistence on the control of methods and materials used in Montessori education led to its reputation in educational circles in the United States as rigid and inflexible. "As a result, the Montessori method had only a slight impact on public schooling and a limited influence on professional teacher education in the United States. However, in the private sector of education, the second wave of Montessorianism, after 1950, has been a resounding success."[108] Some of her ideas, such as the use of manipulatives in teaching math, have been incorporated into mainstream educational theory and practice in the United States in the intervening years.

Montessori education has elements of teaching as spiritual guidance. Aline Wolf reminds us that Montessori herself placed great emphasis on spiritual development. She calls for "renewed attention to this spiritual legacy that may be the most important and far-reaching implication of Montessori education."[109]

Jerome Berryman's Godly Play (and other such programs) are based on contemporary understandings of the Montessori approach. The format of Godly Play includes telling parables and sacred stories and lessons about liturgical acts and symbols, using figures and other props (desert sand in a tray, for example). The props are available in learning boxes for children to retell the stories later. Following the stories the teacher asks "wondering questions" to draw out the child's own meanings and understandings of the material. After the time for questions, each child chooses work before leaving the story circle. The work may be an optional activity, including art responses and reflection, re-telling the story to another child, or even constructive wandering.[110]

Unitarian Universalist adaptations use a wide range of stories and materials. One such program is Spirit Play, developed by Nita Penfold, Ralph Roberts, and Beverly Leute Bruce. It is widely used with specially trained teachers. Lessons and materials are available for use in classrooms. The Spirit Play website notes that the key elements of the program are preparation of the environment and of the teachers, and that this frees children to work at their own pace and on their own issues after an initial lesson or story in "a safe and sacred structure, shepherded by two adults."[111] Goals of Godly Play include modeling how to wonder, showing children how to choose their own work, and organizing the education time to follow the pattern of worship. The snack is called the Feast and represents the Eucharist.[112]

Penfold writes that "Children are thus introduced to the stories of our faith in a concrete way and can wonder about them at their own level of materials, intelligence, and creativity. They are invited to make their own choices at work time. They may go back again and again to the same story until they have absorbed and discovered all that they can."[113]

Both of these programs use a doorkeeper to help create an appropriate ambience for the class. Each might be considered a manifestation of teaching as spiritual guidance. This approach may be used with any curriculum material.

Discovery

Discovery and inquiry were the methods of the multimedia kit era of the UUA (1965–1980) and as such were the approach used in this era. The discovery method is inductive; each learner is challenged to discover the basic concepts of each lesson. However, any number of methods may be used in this approach.

"The discovery method was grounded in the conviction that the most effective learning occurs when children have an opportunity to intuit principles for themselves from experiences in their daily lives," Hollerorth writes. "The discovery method was born out of the rejection of a kind of teaching that is always 'telling' children the meaning or the importance of something without providing or trusting the kinds of learning experiences that allow a child's own understandings to emerge gradually over time."[114]

Responding to criticism from those who felt that the discovery method encouraged teachers to manipulate children to "discover" specific ideas, the UUA curriculum developers for the Multimedia Kits moved to "a four-stage educational model, a version of the inquiry method.... [T]he four stages were initiation, interaction, investigation, and internalization. The model affirmed the premise of the discovery method—that effective learning occurs when learners have an opportunity to intuit principles from actual experience—but it encouraged and supported more divergence."[115] The spirit of discovery and inquiry may be seen in the methods suggested for use in our programs.

Teaching for Understanding/Thinking

The concept of teaching for understanding may be implicit in other approaches, but it is worth keeping in mind regardless of one's basic approach. In the introduction to *Teaching for Understanding*, Martha Wiske suggests that a curriculum be organized around "*generative topics* that are central to the subject matter, accessible and interesting to students, and related to the teacher's passions." The formulation of "explicit *understanding goals* that are focused on fundamental ideas and questions in the discipline" and "engaging learners in *performances of understanding* that require them to extend, synthesize, and apply what they know" are considered to be crucial. She also suggests *"on-going assessment,"*[116] which may be done in religious education without tests or grades, by continuing conversation and creative expression of learning.

Chapter Six

How We Teach: Method

"The method is the message."
--Angus H. MacLean

The actual methods and learning activities used in educational programs are of significant importance. Those used in religious education programs in the liberal church ought to be consistent with who we are as a people and what we believe.

In an address to the Universalist Sabbath School Union of Greater Boston in 1951, Angus MacLean suggested that "the method is the message." This statement predates Marshall McLuhan's "the medium is the message"[117] and has echoed down the years as a tenet of religious education philosophy, although not always evident in practice.

MacLean's words proved to be somewhat provocative. Enlarging on his previous remarks in a booklet published by the Unitarian Universalist Association in 1962, he says, "… I am interested in the kind of teaching situation that uses a child's learning energies. Such a situation will permit a significant percentage of time for work with hands, for talk, and free movement whenever any or all of these are called for by the task in hand. It will be a place in which teacher and child can respond to each other in value terms; where one can think freely, where the teacher loves his or her charges and exercises patience and understanding; where much is expected, and life exciting; where a teacher confronts realities, ranging from the grass frog or angleworm to the mysteries of time and eternity, along with the child; where a wisdom-communicating relationship exists."[118] This broad statement of the methods we might use requires some elaboration for the philosophy to be put into practice.

Content is important, of course. "What shall children study?" This question was asked by Fahs in 1952. She devoted a chapter to her response, but this was the gist of it:

> All that quickens sympathetic imagining,
> that awakens sensitivity to other's feelings,
> all that enriches and enlarges understanding of the world;
> all that strengthens courage,
> that adds to the love of living;
> all that leads to developing skills
> needed for democratic participations—
> all these put together are the curriculum
> through which children learn.[119]

In 2015 the emphasis is on thematic, relevant programming. Whatever topics may be deemed appropriate, method remains important.

A variety of teaching methods has been put forth in religious education curriculum materials, but old habits die hard, and new ways of teaching—not fully understood—are often ignored. "While most church teachers understand that the use of interactive learning methods is more effective for learning in the domain of the spirit (emotional, volitional, and intuitive), the majority of teachers still seem to lecture for most of the time they are with their learners," writes Israel Galindo.[120] If volunteer teachers are made aware of the many methods available to them, and shown how to use them in the classroom, this need not be the case.

Lack of understanding of students' attention spans may lead to spending the entire class time on one type of activity. Fifteen to twenty minutes on one activity is appropriate for older children and youth, but shorter periods of time may be needed for the very youngest. Having an extensive fund of methods to choose from may be helpful for those who develop curriculum materials, direct programs, and create plans for lessons.

Seven Categories of Teaching Methods

The seven suggested categories of teaching methods encompass a wide variety of possibilities for learning activities for faith development. Some speak for themselves. Others call for explanation or description. While they do not correspond precisely with the eight (or eight and one-half) intelligences, using all of these methods will appeal to participants with different intelligences and encourage them to try new ways of learning. When planning specific learning activities, keep in mind your goals for the participants. When using a printed (or online) curriculum guide, be sure you understand the goals of each activity, especially if choosing between options. When designing your own lesson plan, state goals in terms of the learners' experience. For example, in *Special Times* goals for participants in a session on the Sabbath include: "To discover the origins of Shabbat/Sabbath as told in the biblical story." This is accomplished through hearing about the story, hearing the biblical story, hearing variations of the story (Steven Mitchell's *The Creation* and a poem); conversation about the story; and retelling the story through working together to create a mural.[121] The goal may be as simple as this learning objective from Session One of Richard Kimball's online curriculum *Amazing Grace Field Test. Session One*: "Hear the theme song 'Amazing Grace.'"[122]

The categories are:

- Storytelling, and Other Presentations That Engage the Learner—dramatic or musical performances, videos, reading aloud (by the teacher or a helper) of poetry or short works of literary merit, and (yes, sometimes) lecture. The verbal-linguistic learner will benefit from storytelling and the musical-rhythmic from musical performances.
- Creative Expression Opportunities—art response: painting, drawing, collages; bead work, clay work, dance, drama, movement, music making, needlework, origami, photography and videography, singing, puppetry, woodworking, writing.
- These activities are most effective used in the context of the lesson for the day, giving learners an opportunity to tell and retell their learnings as they incorporate them into their being. They may, however, be used at any time appropriately. Most intelligences will enjoy some of these.
- Play—block building and other construction, games (especially collaborative ones), puzzles, costume boxes, and role-playing. Construction activities appeal to the logical-mathematical intelligences, and all group work or play to the interpersonal. Active play, movement, and dance appeal to the kinesthetic learner.
- Discourse—conversation, dialogue, discussion, evocative questions, query. Verbal-linguistic learners are in their element with discourse, but it has appeal for interpersonal learners as well as others.
- Centers or Stations for Learning—a variety of experiences and activities. Providing more than one center, and more than one type of activity, allows choice; participants may self-select for their preferred activities and subject interests, thus appealing to many intelligences. For example, the

simple act of moving about the room appeals to the bodily-kinestethic learner.

- Real World Experiences—field trips, food preparation, group investigations, ritual, service and social projects, mission trips, workshops, nature walks, gardening. While much of religious education may be experiential, experiences that occur in the realm of everyday life, belong in this category. Most if not all of the intelligences will be engaged in planning, carrying out, and reflecting on these activities.

- Reflection and Meditation—coloring mandalas, guided imagery and meditation, labyrinths (miniature and full-size), rock balancing (well supervised for children). Activities involving patterns (coloring mandalas and walking labyrinths—miniature and full size) should appeal to the logical-mathematical learner. Rock balancing, when done quietly by individuals or small groups provides an opportunity for kinesthetic learners (and all active people) to use large muscles in concert with a quiet, meditative activity. Most activities in this category will be especially valued by the intrapersonal learner. Reflecting on all activities and experiences is a significant aspect of learning.

A chapter on each of these categories of teaching methods follows, in Part Two.

Chapter Seven

How We Organize: Models and Structures

"Structures are restraints—a way of limiting."
—Corita Kent

"What you can build within restraints and structures is almost limitless. You will be forced by them to open up and see things within these limits, things you might have passed over if you had been 'free' to wander the world or do anything you felt like doing," says artist educator Corita Kent. "Was it Emerson who said he needed only his own backyard to discover all about the world?"[123]

From the many structures, or models, available to us for learning and teaching, the dominant one for religious education programs has been the school: closely graded "classes," texts (or curriculum guides and story books) written for a narrow age range, and teachers whose role has been seen as imparting knowledge to those younger and/or less knowledgeable.

Other possible models—places where intentional learning and teaching take place—include home, library, museum, and church (or religious institution). Most early learning takes place in the home, and religious beliefs, attitudes, and values are formed there.

Questions are posed (and may be answered) when they occur, explanations are given as the need arises, and stories (from the family or from the tradition) are told when they seem pertinent. Informal times together produce shared experiences for all ages to reflect on in days (and years) to come.

The library (or media center, in contemporary parlance) has books and other resources, quiet places for research, and storytellers. Modern museums have guides to show and explain materials and to ask and answer questions. Many have hands-on materials and learning boxes for exploration. Library and museum education methods may be utilized in faith development programs to meet the needs and interests of individuals and to better accommodate visitors and occasional attendees. In an interview in *Educational Leadership*, Howard Gardner suggests a children's museum approach to teaching and learning: "They are places where kids can find things that interest them and explore these things at their own pace and in their own way," adding that it broadens our notion of what children are like, and what they can do.[124]

The church offers the historical model of all ages in worship together, church suppers and singing schools, camp meetings, children sleeping on pallets on the floor as services go on into the night. Congregational worship is a staple of most faiths, and young as well as old are often included.

Some years ago Dorothy Spoerl described a proposal made by a religious educator in one Unitarian Universalist congregation that was turned down cold. It involved elimination of age-level and grade-level classes for children and adoption of a "program of interest groups in which any child might enroll if he chose to do so...there could be a dance group; an art studio with a wide variety of available media; a dramatic group; a science corner or a laboratory where children could follow the dictates of their own curiosity; a library filled with many books which children could read, or from which they could be read to."[125] Happily, this kind of approach is no longer likely to be frowned upon.

The structural models most frequently in use or under discussion for children's religious education in the early twenty-first century are these: classroom based, home and family education, religious education without walls, rotation (originally called workshop rotation), and worship-education. Any may be used with closely graded, loosely graded, mixed age, or multigenerational groupings. Any may be used with either vertical "pillars" content or horizontal multi-year "themes" content. Any may utilize a wide variety of teaching methods and learning activities.

Classroom Based

This is the most familiar of all structures for religious education programming. It's sometimes called a self-contained classroom. While it may suggest a traditional Sunday School to some, the structure in itself does not imply any particular method of instruction or theoretical model. Participants may be grouped by any method—age, gender, interest, or random assignment. The room may be arranged in a variety of ways, including as an open classroom with learning centers or stations. Montessori inspired programs are classroom based. Many innovative and exciting methods of teaching can be, and have been, used in the classroom setting. Among these are Small Group Ministry, discussion groups, art programs, and many others.

Participants have a sense of being at home in the congregation when they meet in the same place most of the time, especially if they are able to post their own materials and projects. Problems arise when the classrooms are too small or too full of furniture (often inappropriate for the planned activities), and thus don't allow participants and leaders to move about.

When rooms are set up for other purposes, religious education groups have to contend with many distractions and may not develop a sense of ownership of their space. If space is shared with other schools, it is better if a neutral setting can be maintained.

Home and Family Education

Home is the most natural of learning environments. Here people of all ages work, play, and learn together, without regard to whether learning is planned. Most religious education of children takes place in the home; once almost all of a child's education took place there. Today, as many parents teach their children at home, it seems natural for them to recognize their role in religious teaching as well. Ideally home and congregation will offer complementary religious teaching. Congregations may support families by providing resources, classes, and groups to help parents clarify their own values and learn more about their religious heritage, and many do.

Celebration of life's events occur in the home, as do experiences dealing with birth, injuries, illness, and death—all rich opportunities for sharing faith. The building of rituals connected with birthdays, holidays, and other occasions offer parents and children alike a chance to talk about their feelings, understandings, and beliefs regarding important occasions and concerns.

Families of all faiths have customs and traditions that provide at least somewhat formal learning opportunities for sharing faith. The Seder and other Jewish home festivals have long been an important component of religious education that takes place within the context of the family. These have been important in keeping the faith alive when public religious observance was not possible. Christian practice has included family devotions, Bible lessons, prayer, and song. Mormons have Family Home Night, one night during the week when the whole family is sure to spend one evening together. Muslim, Hindu, and Buddhist families, as well as others, observe aspects of religious celebrations together, at home.

Usually home and family religious education will be done in concert with congregational offerings, but for families who do not live near a congregation or who participate in small congregations with very few children, this may be the primary (or only) structure for religious growth and learning. The Church of the Larger Fellowship (CLF) offers resources for such situations.

Religious Education Without Walls

"Way Cool Sunday School," developed by Greg Stewart and others at the Second Unitarian Universalist Church in Chicago, is the best known of this model of religious education programming. Elements of this structure had been used previously for special spring programs or "mini-mesters" and in some cases at intervals throughout the years. This plan is related to the concept in secular education of "schools without walls."

Writing about it in *Essex Conversations*, Stewart says:

> ...we put lived experience before the dissemination of information, took Sunday School out of the church's basement and into the city's streets, eliminated age divisions, used curricula as a resource rather than a recipe, intentionally invited (and transported) non-UU children to Sunday School from area shelter and group homes—yes, we became both missionaries and evangelists—and we confused social action with religious education. We called this approach "Way Cool Sunday School."[126]

Stewart noted wryly that he had "got hold of the wrong reading list," referring to the philosophical readings generally recommended by Unitarian Universalist religious educators, and tried to put into practice what he read there. "Not knowing any better," he said, "I took them seriously." One might guess that there was a somewhat chilly response to his approach in the broader religious education community to bring forth this tongue-in-cheek comment. The program was well received at the Second Unitarian Church, however, and has been adopted (and adapted) by other congregations. It is described on the UUA website as "critically acclaimed...an outside-of-the-box experientially based liberal religious education program."

We might look at Stewart's experience through the lens of shared praxis: he read the Community Story, had a dialogue between the

Community Story and Vision and his own story and vision, and his Faith Response for the Future was Way Cool Sunday School. The program includes some variation of this pattern: first Sunday of the month, all-children worship; second and third Sundays, age-based classes; fourth Sunday, social action projects, and—if there is a fifth Sunday: exploring spirituality through the arts.

Distance education is another type of religious education without walls. The use of computers for webinars and teleconferencing, email, group chats, reading, and viewing videos may play a larger role in religious education programs in the future. The Unitarian Universalist College of Social Justice is an example of such a program for adults, offering education and service work in the field.

Rotation

Melissa Armstrong-Hansche and Neil MacQueen introduce and describe this way of structuring programming in their book *Workshop Rotation*.[127] MacQueen posts this on their website:

> The Workshop Rotation Model in brief: 1. Re-organize your classrooms into creative "workshops," including: Art, Drama, Games, Computer, Video and more. You choose. 2. Rotate your grade groups into a new workshop each week. 3. All the workshops teach the same Bible story for a 4 to 6 "rotation." 4. Teachers *stay put* in the workshop teaching the same lesson each week to a new group. 5. The story gets explored and learned in-depth through a variety of creative teaching mediums. The kids look forward to a different learning experience, teacher, and room each week. The teachers don't have to plan a new lesson each week. Instead, they plan once every four or five weeks, modifying their basic lesson each week for a slightly different age group, and getting better and more creative as the weeks pass.[128]

Obviously most Unitarian Universalist congregations using this model will not teach only "major Bible stories," but any content may be used with rotation of workshops. Slightly different versions of the story may be used in each workshop for variety's sake. Some years ago both Makanah Morriss and September Gerety reported on the UUA's Reach-list their good results using this model with a "pillars" curriculum plan in Cheyenne, Wyoming. They and others have stressed the importance of having "journey guides" with each group as they move through different workshops, providing a continuity of leadership. In other congregations, it is each group's "teacher" who goes with the children each week and those facilitating the workshops are the "workshop leaders." Having journey guides or regular teachers provides continuity of adult leadership, especially important when the children move to a different room each week.

Religious educator Jude Henzy responded to concerns about the rotation model approach in an article published in UU Faith Works, Summer/Fall 2003, saying that children explore "concepts and stories through child-friendly multi-media workshops: an art workshop, drama, music, games, puppets, story telling, computers and other educational media…. The teachers in each workshop lead the same workshop for all five weeks to different children. This approach honors the various learning styles in participants and matches teachers' interests to the different ways of learning. The theory is that the method is the message. While this model covers curriculum content, it focuses more on helping children learn the concept of caring for the earth by creating a play or story about it; others will resonate, if you will, with songs and music on the topic; still others will need to use art, science, or physical movement activities."

The exploration of the same story through different mediums over a period of time is not new to us. The workshop approach is related to learning centers or learning stations on a larger scale, and has often been used in special programs such as spring festivals or "mini-mesters." Library and museum education approaches are evident in different manifestations of this model: use of storytellers, resources, guides, hands-on exhibits, audio-visuals.

In the book *Workshop Wonders*, Mickie O'Donnell and Vickie Bare call this kind of program "the multidimensional learning" model and suggest workshop rooms as follows: storytelling, Bible skills and games, art, music/movement, science and cooking lab, computer, drama/puppetry and audio-visual.[129] They say "It's about transformation, not information."[130]

Worship-Education

Dorothy Henderson describes a worship-education program in an article "Worship and Sunday School: Which model is best for your congregation?" She says, "All ages gather in worship for 20 minutes; for 30 minutes everyone goes to an age-graded educational program with coffee and juice; all ages gather for worship again for 20 minutes." Among the advantages she lists are: it encourages adult learning and provides children with more worship opportunities; it allows people to bring learning, ideas, and crafts back with them into the worship time, provides for both all-ages activity and age-graded activity; and that worship is consequently more multi-sensory. Disadvantages she points out are that most resources are not designed for this type of learning so lots of adaptation is needed, and that "this pattern is so unusual for Presbyterians that some may feel threatened."[131] We may imagine that the same holds true for Unitarian Universalists.

James White describes a program he is familiar with in *Intergenerational Religious Education*:

> The basic program model involved: 1) selection of a worship-education theme for a ten-week program; 2) choice of a unit topic or session for each week consistent with the overall theme; 3) beginning each Sunday morning with a time for all ages to pray, sing, and learn together in worship; 4)

effecting a parallel learning time when children (*not* divided by age) have education in the fellowship hall while adults learn about the same topic in the sanctuary; and then at morning's end, 5) reuniting all ages either in the sanctuary, fellowship hall, the courtyard (with coffee and punch), or elsewhere for mutual sharing.[132]

While some congregations have experimented with such a structure, in most cases it has not been multigenerational. As more congregations seek to develop programs that reach across generational lines, this structure may gain favor.

Youth Programming Structures

There are many variations of programming for teens in our congregations, with classes on Sunday morning and occasionally at other times, youth groups meeting Sunday morning or evening, fundraising activities, social service and mission projects, participation in choirs, theatrical productions, and multigenerational activities. Although there are many variations, most seem to fit into one of these organizational structures: Sunday morning classes and youth group are the same, or there is a Sunday morning program of classes with youth group meetings held outside Sunday morning. In the former, one or more Sunday mornings each month may be devoted to planning activities and projects, with classes on other Sundays. In the latter, classes may be held during, before, or after services, with the youth group meeting on Sunday evening or at some other time. Young Religious Unitarian Universalists (YRUU) is the umbrella youth group of the UUA.

All of these configurations include some form of service learning trips or social justice projects.

Our Whole Lives (OWL) and Coming of Age (COA) classes may be held at times other than Sunday morning. Coming of Age and Bridging ceremonies have become a staple in many congregations and are often moving and meaningful. One might question, however, whether sixteen isn't a better age for recognizing a passage into adulthood than thirteen or so.

Adult Program Options

Adult education and faith development programs come in a variety of models: Adult School (with a variety of evening and Saturday classes and workshops), Sunday morning classes, forums, lectures, seminars, weekly evening classes, and retreats among them. Another model is Small Group Ministry, which may also be called covenant groups or connection groups. Some form of this model is the fastest growing movement among us. Some congregations offer this as an option along with more traditional models. Some use a "basic seminary" approach in planning classes; others may engage in social action as educational practice. These latter two approaches were described and expanded on by William Murry and Rebecca Parker at Meadville Lombard Winter Institute in 1999.

As congregations consider which structures or models to develop for religious education, what methods of teaching are to be encouraged, and the content to be explored, there are useful criteria for the process: Are these models, methods, and content congruent with our Unitarian Universalist principles and with the religious education philosophy of our larger movement? And are the strengths and limitations of the congregation taken into account? Such decisions should be made by a broadly inclusive group: parents, congregational leaders, staff, and all who are interested. Older children and youth can participate in the decision-making for their programs.

Chapter Eight

How We Organize: Groupings

"...genuine respect for all ages and truly intergenerational communities are counter-cultural prospects that require institutional transformation to be fully realized."
— Judith Frediani

Mixed age grouping of children and opportunities for multigenerational learning take advantage of the familiar natural groupings found in families, neighborhoods, and congregational settings.

Small congregations (or large congregations with few children) should not even try to have the closely graded classes that have long been the norm in most churches. While these classes work well for learning, they are not the only ones that do. Congregations with eight or ten children ranging in age from four to twelve don't have the option of dividing them into classes; they are a class all by themselves. It is possible to have excellent learning in a class with a wide age range, if it is done well. A sufficient number of adult leaders is desirable for all classes, and many congregational safety policies require two adults in each class. In a mixed age group, having enough mature leaders is essential. One of these leaders should focus on the younger children in the group to maximize their learning and to lessen distractions for older participants.

There should not be so many adults as to outnumber the children, but even if there are only two children, they and two adults may have a good experience together. Unfortunately, many adults have a tendency to think that unless there is a large group one adult is sufficient. One of two teachers might say, "Oh, there are only four children here today, you can go to the service," but if those four are not pretty much the same developmental level, or if there is an accident or some other incident, there may be difficulties.

Some learning activities (listening to stories, simple crafts) work well for all ages; others may need to be adapted to match developmental needs of all participants. Older children help younger ones as needed, and both benefit from the interaction. Each session may have a ritual (lighting a chalice, repeating an affirmation) and a story or presentation appropriate for all ages, with other activities planned for specific age levels (art response, book corner, group jigsaw puzzle related to the theme.) Learning centers or stations are great in mixed age classes, as participants may work independently or in small groups. Some centers should have activities for the oldest in the group, some for the youngest. Some centers may have pencil and paper activities, others crayons and directions that may be given without words. Book corners should have books for all ages, and good readers may be encouraged to read picture books to younger children.

The old "one room schoolhouse" in small towns or rural settings, or groups of children learning together at home, are traditional examples of mixed age groupings. Montessori from the beginning grouped children by a three-year age span.[133]

Lack of numbers is not the only reason for mixing ages in the classroom. Whether in church or secular education, multiage groupings have many advantages. When children are the same age, there is an assumption that they all have the same level of development, but that is not the case. When there is a wide age range, teachers automatically individualize for each child, insuring that each child's experience is more likely to be satisfactory and that real learning may take place. Large congregations often vary their program for part of the year in such a way as to place children of different ages in the same groupings, and sometimes with adults. This illustrates one way in which large churches try to capture some of the advantages of small congregations.

In the past, few materials have been developed for intentional use in such groupings; more are available now than ever before, with several in the UUA's online Tapestry of Faith. Many materials can be adapted for children who are older or younger than the original targeted age group.

Three teachers who are experienced with mixed age groupings in secular schools write "Within these settings, teachers can provide a wide range of activities to meet a diversity of abilities and interests and can accept a variety of performance competencies as valid."[134] They characterize the rationale for such grouping as "meeting students' individual needs" and say that the focus is on the individual and that learning is activity-based and hands-on.[135] "Students are not spoon-fed material but instead become self-regulating, self-directed learners."[136] The authors point out that this type of grouping is based on principles from cognitive, social learning, sociocultural, psychosocial, and ecological theories.[137]

Portfolios and teacher/child/parent conferences are reflective evaluative elements of such teaching (and learning) that fit well into religious education programs. Indeed, some curriculum resources suggest a cumulative folder or portfolio of student work for a defined period of time. Both of these provide an important link between home and the educational program. It is ideal that each child senses that both home and congregation are supporting their learning.

Jill Ostrow writes about her public school mixed age classroom: "Because what we do is meaningful and purposeful, and the children feel invested in what they are working on, visitors see them actively engaged. I have noticed through my years of teaching and observing children that behavior problems usually occur when children are not invested in what they are working on—when it is not meaningful to them."[138]

Mixed age classrooms are often arranged in the most flexible way that size, space, and other uses of the room permit. "The way the furniture is arranged in my room not only encourages choice, it also allows easy access to supplies. The children know where the supplies are, how to get to them, and what is available to them," says Ostrow. "They can get their own paint, find the other materials they want to work with, and file away much of their own work. This is possible because of the way the room is set up and because I encourage them to be independent learners."[139] She points out that such classrooms, "especially like mine that span four years, demonstrate what children are able to do. They also break down barriers of age and gender."[140]

Even though the amount of time available in religious education programming is much less than the typical school day, there is still time for a variety of activities with options. An hour-long class allows for three twenty minute or four fifteen minute time slots for activities. Children need to move around more than adults do, and this type classroom makes that natural and expected.

"Our multiaged classroom is a rich environment," write Penelle Chase and Jane Doan. The children in this class are five to eight years old. "It is rich in activity. It is rich in sociability. It is rich in differences. The talk here is energetic. Ideas ripple through the room. Caring happens naturally. We believe that learning in a multiaged setting is the happiest way to learn."[141]

Multigenerational Learning Opportunities

Multigenerational learning takes place all the time but is seldom planned for or institutionalized. James White's book *Intergenerational Religious Education* suggests six paradigms for such learning in congregations: family groups, weekly class, workshop or event, worship service, worship-education, and the all-congregation camp.[142] Although White defined both terms more precisely in this book, it should be noted that for the most part "intergenerational" and "multigenerational" have been used interchangeably.

Susan Archer, writing in *Essex Conversations,* says, "What I am advocating is putting out a variety of structural models of learning and growing and encouraging congregations to address their needs and think 'outside the box' in response to those needs." She notes that "many structural possibilities exist" and asks "what if there were intergenerational opportunities for religious education that happened before or after Sunday morning worship?... what if religious education took place on Wednesday night following an intergenerational potluck, after which there was a fun (not leader-intensive) intergenerational activity?"[143] Also in *Essex Conversations,* Frediani suggests that "a congregation engaged in lifespan religious education would … be the ultimate committee of the whole: a community in which everyone is seen as teacher and learner." Noting that this kind of community "is no more than a restatement of the goals espoused throughout our ranks," she says, "As a religious organization we are culturally and institutionally resistant to realizing those ideals."[144]

While religious educators clamor for more congregational activities that involve people of all ages, few curriculum materials or resources for planning such learning opportunities have been available, and few congregations have offered educational programs for all ages together. This is changing, and since 2009, the UUA has posted curriculum plans for multigenerational groupings on its website as a component of Tapestry of Faith. A number of congregations now include multigenerational "events and activities" on their calendars. Those with educational components often include centers or stations, to allow for individual and small group activities.

Dorothy Henderson, in her typology of models for Christian education, suggests such a Sunday morning program, followed by intergenerational worship. Advantages that she points out include: families can be together for learning and worship, learning and worship can be closely linked, learners can bring something to worship from the class, and that it encourages positive interaction across ages. She particularly recommends it for small churches, or for churches with only a few children and youth.[145]

Donald and Patricia Griggs suggest occasions for generations learning together: Sunday morning church school, family nights, vacation church school, retreats, and days and seasons of the church year. "On a special Sunday," they write, "it would be possible to have an extended period combining study, worship and fellowship where all ages participate in the same program."[146] Their book, *Generations Learning Together*—a resource book, planning guide, and curriculum resource all in one—was published in 1976, but much of it is valid today.

The book emphasizes the importance of balancing types of activities to provide a variety of experiences for learners: "One session may feature one type of activity more than another, but there should always be some individual, some small group and some large group activities." They point out advantages and disadvantages for each kind of activity. For example, the individual activities allow each person to work at his or her own pace, make choices, and to interact with leaders. The disadvantages may be lack of interaction with other participants and not being challenged by ideas and feelings of others. Small group activities insure that participants are more involved with each other, thereby exposing all to different ideas, feelings, and values, and develop skills of cooperation, negotiation, and planning. Possible disadvantages are that assertive, verbal persons may dominate; children and less assertive adults may withdraw. They point out that activities involving the whole group take less total time and allow all to experience the same thing, but give less attention to each person and do not allow for as much individual choice. "Worship, games, meals, simulation activities and other similar experiences work well when the whole group is together."[147]

It should be noted that "multigenerational learning in the congregation" implies more than two-generation family units getting together. There may be such programs, but "multigenerational" implies a broader context that includes unrelated persons of all ages and generations, as well as families. Although he mostly uses the term "intergenerational" or "IGRE," White's definition is appropriate: "two or more different generations of people in a religious community together learning/growing/living in faith through in-common experiences, parallel learning, contributive occasions, and interactive-sharing." He explains that "if more than three generations are included in an IGRE activity, the more expansive title of *Multigenerational* is in order. In its fullest implementation, the term suggests that preschoolers, grade-school children, young adults, mid-life adults, and senior-age community members would all be in a learning environment together."[148]

"In-common" experiences are those shared by all members of a learning group, such as hearing a story or watching a movie, both of which may have many levels of meaning. "Parallel-learning" activities are those where smaller groups (by age, interest, or some other determining factor) work separately on the same general learning task or topic.[149] These groups share their responses to the experience as a "contributive occasion". These terms correspond with Griggs' large group and small group activities. White defines "interactive sharing" (a fourth step, not always included) as one where "persons are sent toward each other for purposes of interpersonal exchange."[150]

Learning activities from every category of teaching methods may be used in mixed age and multigenerational groupings. In addition to those mentioned previously, leaders may wish to try these: all ages may work together to create murals or group weavings, act out stories, and other expressions of creativity, such as dance and movement activities, while painting, drawing, and working with clay may be done by individuals, in time set aside for "parallel-learning."

Conversation and evocative questions know no age boundaries, nor does play. Collaborative games, puzzles (related to the theme of the class or workshop) and a variety of building projects are playful activities for all ages.

Real World experiences such as social justice projects, field trips, food preparation, group investigations, gardening are best done by a mix of children and adults. Reflective and meditative activities may be done individually (as parallel activities), in small groups, or by the whole group, although when all ages are together much thought will be required to make them suitable for all. Mandala books are available for both children and adults, children and adults can walk labyrinths together, and when children do rock balancing, it's a good idea to have adults present.

Experience suggests that multigenerational activities present some specific problems as well as offering rich rewards. For example, when small, active children and frail or elderly persons are in the same room, special care should be taken to protect the interests and needs of both groups. Careful, purposeful planning may provide separate areas for activities when all are present and not seated quietly for an activity. With this in mind, multigenerational activities can be among the best experiences for all ages.

PART TWO

Chapter Nine

Story, Stories, and Storytelling

"We live in story, like fish in the sea."
--John Dominick Crossan

Once upon a time, a long time ago, people gathered around fires in the dark evening quiet and began the remarkable, unbroken custom of storytelling. They shared understandings of, and wonderings about, life and death and the world around them and related the commonplace and unusual events of their day. This is a significant tradition in our human heritage and we are storytellers all.

Story is the primary content of religious education; conveying story is its primary method. While not all activities in religious education involve stories, there is really no religious education without them. We marvel at the power of stories to help and to heal, to shape and define, to teach, and to entertain. We know too the power of stories to corrupt and damage, if they are false or distorted. In some places only two or three generations ago, parents and teachers alike warned: "Don't you tell me a story!" or "Don't story me, now." Bearing "false tales" is frowned upon everywhere.

There are stories which do not fit neatly into categories of "true" or "not true." This ambivalence may lead us to reject everything for which we cannot provide a rational explanation. But myths, fairy tales, and other fanciful sounding stories may point to truth, without being factual. My father was a teller of tales, some of them of the genre known as "tall tales." His version of how our home town came to be called Grady went something like this: "When the first train came through, the conductor asked what the name of the town was, and the Halls said 'Hall Station' and the Williams family said 'Williamstown.' But the conductor wasn't about to call two stops every time the train came through, so he said they had to choose one name. They just couldn't agree so the conductor suggested they name it after him. The people asked 'Well, what is your name?' and when he said 'Grady,' they said 'Okay. Let's call it Grady.'" For years I assumed that could not really be true, so imagine my surprise when I read an account of a train robbery on that route, quoting none other than Conductor Grady! Another of my father's stories was about the tornado that was so bad the organ from the Methodist Church flew over town playing "Goodbye, My Baby, I'm Gone." Years later I read about the storm in the files of the Arkansas Gazette. The article noted that the organ from the Methodist Church had been found a few days later, all the way on the other side of town. It did not report what tune (if any) it played on the way. These imaginative stories drew on actual events.

We tell the stories of all peoples and may be more likely to use those from other cultures than that in which we live. Myths (whatever the source) often have fanciful elements. When we use such materials we may be asked "Is that true? Did that really happen?" I have been asked such questions by grown ups and by children: Could Elijah really have been fed by ravens? Did the waters really part for Moses? How could God have created everything in seven days? Is the earth really on a turtle's back? Sometimes we can only respond: "That is the story." We may take from it what we will.

Literalism has led to the word "myth" being viewed as false and something to be dispelled. That is far from the real meaning of the word "myth," which my Systematic Theology professor Charles Price called "the native tongue of religion," bearing the same relationship to reality that poetry does to nonfiction. Mythology points to truth, but its telling may not be factual. Myths tell us how things are and how they came to be. John Dominic Crossan says that we should not see myths as "sophisticated lying" or "stories with gods and goddesses," but draws on Claude Levi-Strauss' thesis that "myth performs the specific task of mediating irreducible opposites."[151] This creates a world, or world view, in which to live. Parables, he tells us, contradict, rather than mediate. They subvert world, but only "that world created in and by myth."[152]

In his book *The Dark Interval,* Crossan says that there are five forms of story: myth, apologue or moral tale, action, satire, and parable, with myth and parable defining the limits of story's possibilities. Clearly he is thinking of religious stories (myth, parable) although as he notes, he has taken apologue, action, and satire from Sheldon Sacks' analysis of works of fiction.[153] And he uses examples of comic strips to illustrate each of these. "It is important to see how story itself admits its own creativity, admits that it is creating, and not just describing world ... Story establishes world in myth, defends such established story in apologue, discusses and describes world in action, attacks world in satire, and subverts world in parable." Parables, he says, "are meant to change, not reassure us."[154] He notes that in "parabolic situations there is the structure of expectation on the part of the hearer and there is the structure of expression on the part of the speaker."[155] He pays particular attention to the stories of Jesus, saying that many "are parables as parables have been designed here, not historical allegories and moral example-stories, which is how the traditional interpretation has presented them. These latter would be forms of apologue ... and well on their way towards the polar opposite of what they were originally.[156]

Alice Blair Wesley notes that "the myths belonging to us belong to our whole culture generally. And what liberals now do with the myths of our common culture—how we interpret and tell and transmit them—is more like than different" among liberal Jews,

Catholics, Protestants and others. "Our myths belong to us in particular ways and to others in other particular ways."[157]

This suggests that we teach older children, youth and adults the myths and stories of the Jewish and Christian Bibles, interpreting these stories according to our understanding and based on authentic scholarship. Most biblical material is not suitable for the very young. But there are suitable stories that may give inspiration and encouragement to children. For example, some of the stories attributed to Jesus or told about him: stories of seeds falling on fertile soil and infertile, of lights placed under bushels and lights shining forth, a story of kindness to children and his desire to be with them, a story of a child sharing his loaves and fishes with others.

The myths that create the world we know and live in are those of the Western world, Jewish and Christian among them. These are not, however, the only myths of our culture or of our faith. The American Myth begins with landing of the Pilgrims and is full of larger than life characters, high ideals, and heroic exploits. As religious descendants of the Pilgrims and Puritans, we have a mythology of our own, closely linked to American mythology.

But if we share myths, we offer balance by also sharing parables. We might say the Genesis creation stories are myth, with the theory of evolution providing a parabolic alternative. Many of the folk tales for adults are parabolic, but so too are some that children relate to. In a world where teaching children to share is the norm, the story of the Little Red Hen is a parable. After all, she eats all of the bread herself. But children can see that she did all the work, too. The story of the Prodigal Son is one that older children relate to; who has not felt slighted by a parent, teacher, or caregiver? Children—and adults—may be challenged to reflection by the stories we tell.

Unitarian Universalism is rich in stories that we may share with one another, even as we share our own responses to the stories of the world. Indeed David Bumbaugh has suggested that "we are defined by a common story rather than a common theology, and ... that story has shaped our institutions in significant ways."[158] What is that common story? And where did it come from? I suggest that it is still being written today. It is, and ought to be always, a work in progress. It seems to me that Bumbaugh is talking about the same thing as the Community Story in the shared praxis approach, where learners relate their personal stories and vision to that Community Story and Vision.[159] Palmer's "Big stories" of the discipline apply here.[160]

Bumbaugh writes specifically about our history and heritage, but that common story has many strands, coming from the different sources of our faith and expressed in our principles. The sources we have identified are: direct experience of transcending mystery and wonder, words and deeds of prophetic women and men, wisdom from the world's religions, Jewish and Christian teachings, humanist teachings, and earth centered traditions.[161] This gives us a broad swath of stories from which to choose.

I daresay many of our Unitarian Universalist stories have elements of the mythic and the parabolic, as well as of morality tale, action story, and satire. Most have heard what I call our one Universalist "miracle story." This is the story of disillusioned preacher John Murray, leaving England for the New World, determined to preach no more. When his ship runs aground off New Jersey, he goes ashore in search of food for the company and runs into Thomas Potter who has built a meeting house and is waiting for a preacher such as this. Potter insists that Murray preach and he finally agrees to do so if the wind does not change and permit the ship to leave. The wind does not change, Murray preaches. He then determines to preach the gospel of Universalism in these colonies. He becomes known by some as the Father of Universalism in America.

So far as is known, there *are* no Unitarian miracle stories.

Each congregation has its own story to contribute to the larger story that is our religious movement. The community stories we share, and the personal stories each of us brings to this community of faith, go into the building of our living tradition.

Some curriculum programs are story based, specifically Godly Play and Spirit Play. Tapestry of Faith curricula are rich in stories.

These stories were chosen to meet specific goals and have been field tested and proven to be effective. That does not mean they are necessarily right for your group and your purpose, so feel free to select something else. In some cases, though, you will *have* to select the story to be told.

Stories

"The stories we tell, whether human or divine, mythic or parabolic, order experience, construct meaning, and build community."[162] For this reason, story selection is important. It is especially so when we have a limited amount of time to tell a limited number of stories. What stories may we tell that relate to our community story and give listeners (children, youth, and adults) an opportunity to relate their own personal stories and visions to the story being shared? When we choose stories to share, whether in a classroom with a few children of approximately the same age and developmental level or in the congregational setting with people of all ages, we should be selective.

Many commercial children's books, especially those called picture books, are suitable for use in the program or worship service. Think about possible messages to be taken from a story; each listener may hear an individual message but it is good to be aware of the most likely to be transmitted. It is for this reason a good idea to discuss the story with at least one other person ahead of time. And regardless of the age of the listeners, we don't need to tell them what we think is the moral of the story.

In a congregational worship service it is good if the story relates to the overall theme of the service. Remember that it is a worship experience and should have serious intent. It need not be solemn; a touch of humor is often welcomed. This segment of the service is intended to appeal to children, youth, and adults. Avoid playing to adults, though, especially for laughs. About five minutes is a good length for a story for all ages. The source of the story should be credited.

The best stories have different levels of meaning, so they can be understood by listeners of different ages and stages of development. Remember that many folktales/fairy tales were originally meant for adults so may not really be the most appropriate stories for children. And remember that children's books are selected by adults, so adults may enjoy hearing those stories, too.

It is good for stories used in religious education classes to be used in the congregational service on occasion. The posting online of stories for Tapestry of Faith[163] has made this easier and more likely to happen. Whether they are stories of Jesus or of Martin and Judy, of Gandhi or Martin Luther King Jr., the Buddha or the Pilgrims, John Brown or Olympia Brown, they will be community stories only as they are known to the community as a whole. Especially in the congregational service a story should have resonance for a variety of people. If it is an old, familiar story, even the oldest in the congregation relate to it. If it is an old, familiar story with a twist, so much the better.

More intense stories are better told in the classroom where and when there is an opportunity to process them with caring adults. If told in the congregational setting, children should be seated with their parents or adult caregivers to provide a sense of security.

Storytelling

Most of us tell stories naturally and frequently without giving it much thought, but when called upon to "tell a story" we may see it as a difficult task. Whether in a small group of children or a congregational worship service, telling a story is usually more effective than reading it. Sometimes, however, the language is so much a part of the story that reading it is better. I have learned that if I read a story out loud several times I may then be able to read it as if telling it. When using a picture book, don't depend on the pictures to carry the story, even if it is projected on a large screen. The words are still important!

Concrete objects appeal to children, and to some adults as well. A while back religious educators in the Washington, DC, area published two booklets of ideas for intergenerational worship, all featuring concrete objects. The first one of these involved squeezing all of the toothpaste out of three tubes and then trying to get it back into them. Linda Olson Peebles used this in a service on the importance of choosing our words carefully, as they are so hard to take back.[164] Other objects in the booklets included flowers, stones, hats, shells, glow sticks, paper snowflakes and hearts, jack-o-lanterns and balloons, bells, crayons, pompoms, and a surprising number of apples.[165] The apples bring to mind a memorable service in which the minister, Robert Fraser, ate an entire apple, core and all, while telling a story about an apple. Objects hidden in bags or boxes add an air of mystery as children wonder what might be hidden there. The use of the Wonder Box, in Tapestry of Faith classroom programs, and in congregational worship, is increasingly popular and effective. In the classroom the storyteller may place figures on a flannel board or make a large drawing while telling the story. Puppets, either commercial or made for the occasion, may be used in classroom or worship settings. These may be as simple as odd socks, with or without button or felt eyes attached.

Joseph Bassett, who created the story-based religious education program *Adventures of God's Folk*, suggested to field test teachers as a storytelling aid that as every story has *figures* and *moves*, considering who the figures are, and how they move, will help us tell the story.

In her little book *Getting Started in Storytelling* Sandra Gutridge Harris suggests steps of preparation and practice for making a story your own and learning to tell it to others. In preparation, read it through several times, close your eyes and visualize it, then reduce the story (in writing) to ten sentences, then to five, then to one. Practice telling a bare-bones version, telling the story in front of a mirror, re-writing and modifying it if you wish. She also suggests reading it with a classical music background, recording it, and telling someone a dress-rehearsal version.[166]

In the classroom, opportunities abound for learners to tell and re-tell the stories they hear, through role-play, painting murals, making books, and a variety of other methods. The Rotation model offers a good example of telling and re-telling a story in different ways and making it not only possible but easy for the learners to make the story their own through creative expression. Of course not every story will have that appeal for every student. Careful selection of universal stories will help with this. When a child doesn't want to listen because "we've heard that story lots of times" perhaps that child can help to tell it.

Other Engaging Presentations

Stories are not the only kind of presentation that engage the learner. Dramatic, dance, or musical performances are well-liked and appropriate. If younger ones want to dance during the performance, space may be provided for that. Musical performances may evoke the deepest of emotions and call forth strong feelings. While listening to recorded music (especially short pieces) may have power, live music is more likely to engage listeners/viewers. Recorded music may work well as an accompaniment to dancing or singing simple songs. Older children who play well may enjoy performing for younger ones. Quiet recorded music played as children arrive in the classroom helps to create a calm setting.

The teacher or someone else who reads well may read poetry or short works of literary merit. Videos are popular, but it is important to be selective. Not all popular movies or television shows are good choices. They should be previewed and possible messages discussed by teachers before using them.

Stories and other engaging presentations, while worthwhile in themselves, also offer bountiful material for creative expression on the part of listeners and observers.

Chapter Ten

Creative Expression and the Development of Faith

"Art, metaphor, story, symbolism, music, movement and the other creative arts are powerful tools for religious education."
—Sherry H. Blumberg

The creative potential of the child (or adult) is encouraged and enhanced by engagement with the arts, especially the expressive arts. The purpose of creative expression in the religious education classroom is not to create a pretty or interesting object, although the result may be both beautiful and interesting. The process is what is important, whether in making a picture or working toward solving a problem. "There is an energy in the creative process that belongs in the league of those energies which can uplift, unify, and harmonize in all of us," writes Corita Kent in *Learning by Heart*.[167]

Nita Penfold writes about this energy also: "Creativity is one way in which we can access this life-giving energy and express our spiritual core, our unique feelings, perceptions of wonder and awe, ideas and experiences, back out into the world. It is our birthright as human beings—we are all born creative."[168]

Participants in the UUA's Essex Conversations in 1999 and 2000 were asked for their visions for religious education in the twenty-first century. John Tolley wrote about creativity. In an essay titled *Child's Play*, he says, "To order our conception of how art can serve our educational purpose eliminates the artificial boundaries between child and adult education. The source of our yearning to meet our potential is the inner child seeking order, understanding, and connection. The inner child is our guide whether we are five or ninety-five." He proposes that we give "each child, and our child within, the opportunity to contemplate mystery through intuition, action, and creation." Including reflection in the creative process is important for the development of faith. This helps us in the making of meanings. Tolley says "The very act of creating in image, movement, song, and speech is co-creation with a universe that yearns for our participation."[169]

Many, if not most, religious education programs feature a story or lesson followed by a craft or art project. Often this is not appreciated as creative expression, and if it is a picture or worksheet to color with crayons, it is not! After hearing a story, some participants will want to express their feelings (and re-tell the story) by painting or working with clay; others may wish to sing, make music, or dance the story. Some will want to read the story themselves, or tell it to others in the group. Some may wish to compose a poem or write (or draw) in a journal. Some just want to do "constructive wandering." I take this to mean a child walking around the classroom, observing and obviously thinking about ongoing activities, and not disturbing anyone.[170] If such options are available, you will soon have a busy classroom.

Unfortunately, time, space, and lack of volunteers may limit the possibilities. Many curriculum leader's guides call for a specified craft project or a group activity. Sessions may be thus limited, but even then it is possible to allow opportunities for creative expression—if the project is making construction paper flowers, it's okay to have green flowers with pink stems or bugs drawn on the leaves. Avoid giving children patterns to use unless there is a clear, specific reason for their use, such as when making things that need to fit together. Murals with a touch of graffiti are fine. It is more important for each child to be able to express him/herself than to create a pre-planned outcome.

The significance of this time following the presentation of a theme or topic may become clearer if we re-frame our thinking about it, from "craft activity" to re-telling the story through a variety of activities. Berryman calls this the "art response."[171] When learners create an art response to a story or other presentation, they are doing what Jo Milgrom has identified as "handmade midrash,"[172] the imaginative interpretation of texts through creative, nonverbal means. We usually think of *midrash* as a story told in the Jewish tradition, retelling a biblical story. Milgrom's beautiful book of workshops, illustrated by "handmade midrash," explains the term and the process, where participants re-tell the story "through simple art activities...such as tearing and pasting construction paper or muslin, working with clay, or penciling various kinds of lines to explain a text more fully."[173] She notes that the term *midrash* describes a genre of literature "in which imaginative interpretation discovers biblical meanings that are continually contemporary" and says that the goal of the method "is to awaken and nourish each individual's capacity for the creation of midrash."[174] Milgrom's workshops use biblical material or stories of Jewish life and learning, but the process may be used with any stories.

Sherry Blumberg has described creative midrash thus: it "uses reflection and symbolism to express a person's feelings, thoughts, and responses to a text or a question. The expression is usually nonverbal although some participants need to add the words. The product is not an 'artistic' work, although many are quite beautiful; rather, it is a representation of the soul of the artist, reflecting the creator in new ways."[175] This kind of creative expression is effective with people of all ages. When working with children, don't draw conclusions about the work they have done; instead ask if they would like to tell you about it.

Midrash understood this way may apply to any activity allowing the listener to incorporate the meanings taken from the story and re-tell the story through a creative medium (art work, role play, movement, dance). I think this is what we are doing in religious education at its best.

"A special concern of ours is the release of creativity, and the use of intuitive ideas and perceptions in the area of religious education," wrote Dorothy Spoerl early in our time as a consolidated religious movement.[176] "The real reason for the development of creative activity in religious education is the contribution it can make in the individual as a person."[177] Encouragement of creativity in the work of the classroom helps the person to use creative potential in other aspects of life. This speaks to the connection between the arts, creativity, and spirituality. "The development of the creative potential in the individual can make real differences, recognizable and traceable, in the totality of that person's life." Spoerl says this frees the person to be a self-respecting individual whose creative capacity can give more direction is which to use individual powers, and more strength for doing so.[178]

Materials for Creative Expression

Most classrooms will have space for paper and markers (non-permanent) for children to use at some point in the session. If you cannot have a variety of materials to work with each session, perhaps once a month you can devote an entire morning to creative activity. This may include painting, movement or dance, making music, writing poetry and journaling. If planning to do this, mention it to children in the weeks ahead to help them prepare emotionally and to know that they will have a longer period of time to work on their art responses to the content of the program. It is important to honor work done by even the youngest. Post it for display, file it in a folder or box to keep until the end of the unit, or send it home. It is important not to discard it right away. Unfinished work may be kept to work on at a later date.

Crayons are not the best medium to use for creativity, as they are so familiar and associated with prescribed instructions, such as "Don't color outside the lines." But even they may be used creatively. They work for coloring mandalas with detailing that is not too fine. They may be used for free hand drawing on blank paper. Peeled and broken crayons make good instruments for creative coloring, using the sides as well as the tips. Small broken pieces melted in muffin tins are great for multi-colored crayons. You can do this with or without paper muffin cups, but the cups save a lot of wax removal. When spring cleaning the supply closet collect these crayon stubs and use tiny bits for melting. Place the tin in the sunshine on a hot summer day. Save larger peeled and broken crayons to start the year with. When tempted to give children something to color, give them these to use. (And remember that using blank paper is less time-consuming than copying a worksheet or a page from a coloring book.) Later, brand new wrapped crayons may be added. Some children really love them.

Issues concerning paint in the classroom are understandable. Paints are messy. The use of this most fluid of materials is so important that it is worth making the effort to use paints, with brushes or for finger painting, at times. Outdoors on a nice day foot painting is fun, too. In lieu of paint, the wide variety of non-permanent felt-tip markers available make them a good choice for classroom use. Be sure to have some with medium and broad points, as well as the fine ones used for writing.

Water soluble wax crayons and water color pencils use very little water. They are much easier for children to use and not as messy as water colors with brushes or painting. They work best on water color paper, but you can experiment with other surfaces. These are not cheap but are worth the investment, especially for older children and youth.

Different kinds and sizes of paper are needed for cutting, tearing, folding, pasting, drawing, painting, and collages. Making paper and making books are activities suitable for older children, youth, and adults. Even small children can make simple booklets with lots of adult help. Instructions for making paper, and for making books, are readily available online. A fun idea for little children who are learning about themselves is to draw an outline around their bodies on large pieces of paper and let them decorate with fabric scraps for clothing, yarn for hair, and markers for features. All sorts of "findings" may be of use: yarn of different colors and sizes, beads, thread, buttons, fabric scraps, spools, and small stones may come in handy. Also useful to have available in the classroom: paste, glue, different kinds of tape: transparent, masking, and painter's.

Boxes of different sizes may be used in creative projects, including dioramas, construction, storage for costumes, and story boxes for future use. Items to go in the story boxes--such as clothespin representations of Joseph and his brothers, with all but Joseph dressed in plain fabric—can be made by older children. Wax is needed for candle making. Beeswax and the new soy candle wax are best as there may be allergies in the classroom.

Clay, while hard to prepare and to work with, is a great medium for creative use. If clay isn't a possibility, there are different kinds of modeling compounds you can use, including modeling dough you can make yourself. The children can make their own, if you choose a no-cook recipe. Recipes for making play dough abound on the internet (just search play dough). You might also try salt dough that will harden so that images made from it can be kept.

All of these items are considered supplies; they are used up. Equipment is the term for those items that are used with the materials but aren't used up. Of course they need replacement eventually. This category includes needles, scissors paper cutter, staplers, tape dispensers. One or more cameras should be available for use by participants for photography and making videos. Teachers, parents, or helpers may photograph class activities throughout the year.

Once when I was shopping for beginning of the year supplies, a little boy eyed my shopping cart filled with all sorts of craft materials and asked who I was buying them for. I responded that they were for the children in the church where I worked. He turned to his mother and said, "That's the church I want to go to!"

Other Activities

Some curriculum materials have instructions for writing different forms of poetry. Among those who have written about helping children to write poetry is Kenneth Koch. His *Wishes, Lies and Dreams* has suggestions for class collaborations, poems using lies or talking about colors, writing while listening to music, "I Used To/But Now," and many others. Each form is illustrated by poems written by school children.[179] Children too young to write, or who have difficulty writing, may wish to dictate to a teacher or helper.

Reflective writing at the end of a session, either in silence or accompanied by quiet music is effective for older children, youth, and adults. This may be done in a journal, on loose leaf paper, or on a computer. No one's journal should be read without permission, and the child may not wish to have it sent home. Whatever writing is done should not be judged, corrected, or changed by teachers. It's fine to ask questions about the work that may lead to changes being made if material is to be disseminated in some form. Students in one theological school class were offered a time for reflective writing at the end of each session, but several students did not write anything and one insisted on talking. When mandalas, markers, origami paper and other supplies were brought in for possible use in this reflective time, the group eagerly used them as they reflected on the morning. At the end of the semester, one student said "I never want to take another theological school class without 'crafts'!"

Still photography and videos are good projects for participants when they fit in with the topic of the program. Making a class scrapbook is a good idea. Children may look at it from week to week and after the class ends it may be preserved for the archives. For historical purposes it is good to name participants, but parents should probably be asked for approval if including children's names. If pictures are on bulletin boards where the public may see them names should not be included.

Role-play, dramatic readings, simple plays, and pageants offer opportunities for a different kind of creative expression. Having a costume box or wardrobe available enhances these activities. Puppet play may also be used expressively, using purchased puppets or those made by participants themselves. Older children may do creative projects using photography.

Music making, movement, singing, dancing—all of these may be creative responses to the story or lesson or as planned activities in their own right. If you plan to play live or recorded music while participants paint, work with clay, or do other creative work, selection is important. Choose something that *feels* appropriate to the sense of the story. The youngest children are likely to respond spontaneously with movement or dance. Movement activities (with or without music) can fit into any curriculum. It is great to have equipment for making music in every classroom—something simple like bells or a tambourine, an assortment of rhythm instruments, or an autoharp, a keyboard, a piano.

Creative activities need not be used only for responding to the story or lesson, but are appropriate for their own sake. They relate closely to activities in the next chapter, which focuses on play.

Chapter Eleven

Learning Through Play

"Play is the forerunner of religion."
—Horace Bushnell

Play is not an alternative to learning, but rather the most vital means of learning for young children. It is through play that children learn most readily. The infant learns that absence does not mean abandonment by playing Peek-a-Boo. Most toddlers enjoy finger games and songs. (Where *is* Thumbkin?) They may squeal with delight through innumerable rounds of This Little Piggy. Preschoolers play Let's Pretend, by themselves or with others. "You be the baby and I'll be the mommy (or the daddy)," for example, is a popular refrain, as is "I'm a puppy (or kitty)." This trying on of different identities helps the child deal with reality through imaginative activities. Acting out stories is a natural progression, and one three year old directed this grandmother through countless re-enactments of the story of Little Red Riding Hood. Role-playing gives older children an opportunity to step into another's shoes when Let's Pretend is too babyish. They may like to play School and experience the power and authority of the teacher.

Play sometimes has been called "the work of children," perhaps to legitimize it. Through the years most play was essentially free form, organized by the children involved. One exception was in early childhood classrooms where free play was the order for much of the day. Few have questioned the value of free play for little children until recently. Now many early childhood programs focus on readiness for reading and arithmetic, limiting the time children have for the important activity of play. This makes it even more important that religious education programs offer opportunities for play.

Young children should have time to play and access to dolls, stuffed animals, kitchen equipment, blocks, trucks, cars, and balls. An example of a preschool religious education program offering free play to begin every session is Katie Covey's *Chalice Children*.[180] In addition, children use blocks to create a neighborhood in one session of this program. Play is included in other Tapestry of Faith programs for children: *World of Wonder, Moral Tales* and *Toolbox for Faith* among them.

Even those who believe in the importance of free, spontaneous play for the very young child may have little tolerance for such activity as the child grows older. Older children are often directed into organized, competitive sports. Some may focus all their attention on computer activities or practice the art of being bored. They still need time and space for active, self-directed play and time for day dreaming, a form of mental play. Many children (and youth) enjoy cooperative games, especially when working in teams. Much social learning and community building may occur through play, especially active, outdoor play.

Board games, commercial or teacher-made, interest many children. Older children may make their own board games to suit the theme of the class, using poster board. Another option is to use the inside of a file folder which can be easily folded and filed away when not in use. Playing pieces may be purchased, but small stones, buttons, and coins work just as well.

Thomas Armstrong suggests specific games that appeal to the different intelligences, although not all of them are readily available.

- Linguistic—Scrabble
- Logical-mathematical—Monopoly
- Spatial—Pictionary
- Bodily-kinesthetic—Twister
- Musical—Encore
- Interpersonal—Family Feud
- Intrapersonal—The Ungame
- Naturalist—Frank's Zoo.[181]

The costume box is an important fixture in the classroom. For older children studying biblical material, it may contain castoffs from the Christmas pageant. The early childhood program's costume box may be equipped with hats, clip on ties, brief cases and ladies' purses, to be used as they play at being grown up. I once witnessed a group of four year olds put on hats and pick up briefcases and bags. When asked where they were going, they said "to a meeting." One child added, "You'll be asleep when we get home. It will be very late."

When children (of any age) arrive at different times, invite them into the space in a playful way, with puzzles or simple games that take only a couple of minutes to play placed on tables for easy access. A block corner or sturdy village of doll houses and small people or animals to populate them works well, also. A puzzle and game corner might be in every classroom, or in an area accessible to all classes. Jigsaw puzzles may be found (or made) to fit in with almost any curriculum topic or theme. Many catalogs have blank puzzle forms to draw pictures or write words on. You may also have photographs made into puzzles. Some examples are: a puzzle with a picture of the congregation's meeting place; a group picture of the class; shells, turtles, and houses for *Creating Home*.[182] Session Four of that curriculum includes a matching puzzle.

The Importance of Play

As testimony to the significance of play for healthy human development, Principle Seven of the United Nations Declaration of the Rights of the Child states that "The child shall have full opportunity for play and recreation, which should be directed to the same purposes as education."[183]

Imaginative activities such as creative writing, putting together a story as a group, "playing" with clay or other art materials is another way to engage the playful spirit of the child (or the adult). "Watch a child when she is drawing or painting," writes Corita Kent. "You will see a worried look on her face—a look of intense concentration. Is she working or playing?"[184]

Creating environments for meaningful play is important for young children, but people of all ages benefit from play. "Play is a catalyst for learning at any age," according to the National Institute of Play. "The science of play is validating what gifted educators … have long been practicing and advocating. When students have fun at learning, they continue to pursue it for its own sake. It is how nature assured us how to learn about the world and our places in it. At any age, play acts to retain and enhance meaningful context, and optimizes the learning process. All gifted parents, master teachers, and wise executives know this."[185] Adults play for many important reasons: building community, keeping the mind sharp, and keeping close the ones you love, says Stuart Brown, director of the Institute.[186] He also asserts that pleasurable, purposeless activity prevents violence and promotes trust, empathy, and adaptability to life's complications.

The UUA's adult curriculum *Principled Commitment*, includes a session devoted to play. "We like to laugh, play games, and use our imagination and creativity throughout our lives," say the authors. "In relationships, a spirit of playfulness can ease tensions, build intimacy, facilitate connection, help us solve problems, and lower stress. Today we'll look at some ways in which we can bring the spirit of play into our relationships to help them thrive."[187]

Sacred Play

Play is an important component of faith development. Sacred Play and Godly Play are terms that have been used in teaching liturgy to children. Catholic, Protestant, and Orthodox liturgists explored practical and theoretical aspects of planning and carrying out liturgies for children in a book entitled *The Sacred Play of Children*.[188] In the introduction Thomas Ryan says "This is more than narrow education. This is the formation of open hearts. Thus sacred play educates at deep levels. It forms young and old as the People of God."[189] Jerome Berryman begins his book *Godly Play* thus: "Godly play has something in common with all play. The pleasure of it comes from the act of playing itself. Play is re-creation. The enormous range and depth of such re-creation, however, is too often overlooked. Many see playing as a superficial or trivial act, but I see it as a life-giving act. It makes us young when we are old and matures us when we are young."[190]

While Unitarian Universalists are less likely to focus on liturgy, the re-creative aspect of play is sufficient reason for including it in faith development programs.

The idea of play as religious learning is not a new one. The 1876 edition of Horace Bushnell's *Christian Nurture*, devoted a chapter to "Play and Pastimes, Holidays and Sundays." Referring to a passage from the book of Zechariah, he says, "that religion loves too much the plays and pleasures of childhood, to limit or suppress them by any kind of needless austerity." He sees play as the natural and God-given state of childhood. "As play is the forerunner of religion, so religion is to be the friend of play; to love its free motion, its happy scenes, its voices of glee, and never, by any needless austerities of control, seek to hamper and shorten its pleasures."[191] He goes so far as to say that very young children should be allowed to play on

Sunday although some of the "noisier playthings" might be taken away, or "that he have a distinct Sunday set of playthings; such as may represent points of religious history, or associate religious ideas, abundance of which can be selected from any variety store without difficulty."[192] The popular Noah's Ark is an example of a "distinct Sunday plaything."

Sophia Fahs wrote this about play (remember that "his" was generic and meant to include everyone in the 1950s): "For the young child, his play is a away of experimenting with life, of digging deeper and exploring more widely into its meaning. A child's toys are his library, and his nursery and playground are his laboratories. His play is serious business—enjoyable, yes, but all-absorbing and filled with meaning." She goes on: "In his play the child tries to learn to how it feels to be somebody else, or he sets himself the task of reliving parts of his own experiences in order to know himself and others better."[193]

The faith community may also provide time, space, some basic equipment, and guidance for play, just for the fun of it, indoors or outside. This may be at the congregation's facility or at a retreat center or campsite. In planning opportunities to play for all ages, but especially for the older population, be aware of the capabilities of the least fit person in the group. In classes and organized groups, any games chosen should be accessible to everyone in the group. In less structured settings, such as a church retreat, activities that not all may participate in the are fine, as long as there are other options available.

Chapter Twelve

Discourse

"Insofar as teaching refers to interaction in the human community, teaching is always a form of conversation."
—Gabriel Moran

Much of what takes place in the classroom and other religious education programming can be seen as a form of discourse. The Random House Dictionary defines discourse as "communication of thought by words; talk; conversation; a formal discussion of a subject in speech or writing, as a dissertation, treatise, sermon, etc."[194] This definition encompasses the conversational method, dialogue, discussion (guided or free-for-all), evocative questions that encourage a sense of wonder, query, informational questions, and some answers. It is important to consider that *listening* is an important aspect of teaching and learning through discourse.

Conversation

Conversation is more likely to produce authentic sharing than formal discussion. This is true for all ages, not just for little children. Building on the work of Margret Buchmann, Glen Fielding says, in a journal article about curriculum development, that Buchmann "distinguishes conversation from the more conclusion-driven and deliberative form of exchange associated with argumentation and debate. Conversation, she suggests, evokes and clarifies people's feelings, perceptions images, and thoughts; it does not subject them to critical scrutiny or debate. As an open, nonjudgmental kind of discussion, conversation facilitates the discovery of ideas and the development of a sense of intellectual and emotional partnership."[195]

Bronson Alcott no doubt shocked some with his teaching method recorded as *Conversations on the Gospels* nearly two centuries ago, demonstrating his belief that human nature is basically good. He taught religion to children through what he called "conversation," although he more specifically stated that education was "the art of asking apt and fit questions."[196] One can imagine that he was trying to improve on the oft-reviled catechism.

In her more recent *Conversations With Children,* Edith Hunter says that what she means by conversation is "a give-and-take of ideas either between a few individuals or between a leader and a group."[197] This describes the conversational approach very well. The book is composed of essays that recall actual conversations with children, her own and others, with comments and suggestions for use in the classroom. Together these form the basis for teachers to engage children in conversation on a particular topic. She points out the necessity of truly listening to children if we wish to have meaningful conversations with them.[198] Among the topics she proposes for conversation are curiosity, times past, the natural world, senses and feelings, ethics, and universals. This last category includes conversations about birth and death.

It is through conversation that teachers and learners may get to know one another. Teachers need not (and should not) answer intrusive personal questions and should be thoughtful about what information is appropriate to share. Nor should they ask intrusive questions nor insist on answers from anyone—the option to "pass" should always be available.

Providing resources for use in the home is an important part of Tapestry programs. Every "Taking it Home" for kindergarten through fifth grade has a "Talk About It" section that could lead to conversation or discussion, depending on how the parents use it. The sixth grade "Taking it Home" pages have suggestions for conversations with friends and family.

Deep Listening

Deep listening is a form of active, rather than passive, listening, as it requires focus and attention. Listeners are expected to truly hear what another is saying, rather than commenting or thinking about what to say next. Deep listening is implied whenever one person speaks for a prescribed amount of time and one or more others listen with quiet concentration and without interrupting. *Principled Commitment*, a Tapestry of Faith adult program provides instructions for listening for "what is deep inside, needing to be expressed, yet often ignored." They suggest using Kay Lindahl's three elements of deep listening: silence, reflection, and presence.[199]

Dialogue and Discussion

David Bohm notes a meaning of the word "dialogue" that is somewhat different from what is more commonly understood: "The derivations of words often help to suggest a deeper meaning. 'Dialogue' comes from the Greek word *dialogos*. *Logos* means 'the word,' or in our case we would think of the 'meaning of the word.' And *dia* means 'through' — it doesn't mean 'two.' A dialogue can be among any number of people. ... The picture or image that this derivation suggests is of a *stream of meaning* flowing among and through us and between us. This will make possible a flow of meaning in the whole group, out of which may emerge some new understanding." This is the premise of a method often used in youth and adult groups, and it may be used successfully with older children, as well. Although Bohm is suggesting something that may be more like the dialogue in Small Group Ministry, where groups continue for a while and relationships deepen, the process is the same for shorter term groups.

In such dialogue, space is given for everyone to speak, and listening to each person is vital. "The object of a dialogue is not to analyze things," writes Bohm, "or to win an argument, or to exchange opinions. Rather, it is to suspend your opinions and to look at the opinions—to listen to everybody's opinions, to suspend them, and to see what all that means." In contrast, Bohm notes that discussion has the same root as percussion and concussion and that it really means "to break things up."[200] The object of a discussion is to analyze things, to look at different sides of an issue, to argue or debate informally, with the aim of reaching a conclusion. Brainstorming, where people in a group call out responses to a question or issue quickly and without taking time to listen to others, may lead to further discussion toward decision making. Panel discussions feature two or more presenters who may offer different points of view. Audience participation is usual after the presentations. All forms of discussion play a role in decision making for action.

Questions

Berryman uses "Wondering Questions" in Godly Play. After the story the storyteller may say something like: "I wonder what this could really be?" and when a child responds "a tree," asks "I am wondering what more it could be?"[201] There are other evocative questions we might ask: "Who in this story might be something like you?" or "How did this story made you feel?" If you choose to ask questions requiring factual answers, be prepared to provide the answer if no one else does. It isn't fair to leave that kind of question hanging in the air, although the wondering questions may linger.

Those who tell the story in the congregational worship service often ask questions to involve children in the story. This is tricky. One memorable Advent Sunday, I asked, "Have you ever had to wait a really long time for something?"—expecting the usual "Christmas," "my birthday," or "for a new baby"—but instead hearing child after child say something like "to see the doctor in the emergency room." They finally got around to the usual responses, but not before the minister, Vanessa Rush Southern, asked with mock seriousness, "Should I be calling child services?"

Don't ask questions if you don't want to hear the answers. And questions with only one answer (and that one known only to you) are not a good idea. "Wrong" answers often lead to laughter that makes children (or adults, if at their expense) feel de-valued. Responses that might be easily clarified in a classroom setting are more difficult to clarify in congregational worship. Children's honest answers may sometimes seem hilarious to some adults.

A distressing example of this took place one morning in the time for all ages. I talked about different ideas about God, and then asked "What thoughts do you have about God, or what have you heard others say about God?" One little girl, clearly delighted with the question and thinking about the white cloth draped on a crucifix she had seen, confidently responded "God wears a diaper!" This caused the congregation to erupt with laughter, so loud that she appeared crushed and several children were obviously frightened. Dismayed, I surveyed this congregation I knew and loved and demanded, "Can any among you say with certainty that God does *not* wear a diaper?" Quiet ensued and I thanked her for the response and she was able to regain her composure. The group of children relaxed, and we went on with the service.

The best kind of questions may be evocative ones that ask listeners to think about the feelings roused by the story, helping them to articulate meanings for themselves.

Children's Questions

Teachers are not the only ones who will ask questions in the faith development program. Children have plenty of their own. Whole books have been written regarding some of their questions. Among these is one by Hunter in which she notes that "children ask perplexing questions."[202] They do, indeed. When about twenty-five years of age, I was asked by a second grader pointing to a picture of a churn, "What is this?" After I told him, he asked "How does it work?" My explanation must have been pretty good, because his next question was, "Were you an old churn lady, in the olden days?"

Informational questions require an honest answer. Some of these will be easily provided. Others really call for opinions. The only honest answer may be "I don't know" or "I think so-and-so but others disagree." When each of my children asked the Santa Claus question, I responded with "What do you think?" This worked for a while, but each of them finally said, "I don't want to tell you what I think; I want to know the truth."

After any presentation, listeners may have questions. It is better to ask "What are your questions?" than "Do you have any questions?" The latter may imply that if you were listening you would not, while the former assumes you will want to know more.

Quizzes and Guessing Games may be popular with some learners, if not framed as a "test" of knowledge. Games modeled after the television show "Jeopardy," where the answer is given and participants provide the questions, is popular with older children. So is Trivial Pursuit, either the commercial game or versions created to go with the theme of classes.

Query

In the Quaker tradition *query* is the term used for questions used for reflection and spiritual exercises. Deborah Kahn describes an exercise included in a class on *Query as a Spiritual Discipline*, where participants wrote and shared their answers to these questions: "Who am I? How do I know? Who or what is in charge? What is my purpose in life? What does my death mean?" Kahn says that the responses of others linger in her thoughts and memory, "awakening my consciousness…still creating new ways that I am thinking about what is everlastingly right and good." She notes that through creative interchange, sharing meanings and value, new meaning and value come into the world. "Universal creativity and transformation continue."[203]

Lectures and Sermons

As noted earlier, lectures play a role when someone with authoritative knowledge and an engaging manner of speaking is available to share with older children, teens, or adults. Gabriel Moran says: "For teaching by lecture the speaker and the text need a ritualized setting. The listeners need to be capable of appreciating well-written prose delivered with a forceful style. The author needs to speak words that come from the depth of the self. The aim of a lecture is to change, however imperceptibly, the listener's actions as a human being." He suggests that lecturing to a three-year-old is futile, but that a seven-year-old might benefit from a one-minute lecture.[204]

Moran also says that "when all the conditions are right, a sermon can be among the most powerful forms of teaching."[205] The conditions he suggests are that the preacher speaks to a community from a text that expresses the community belief. When religious education groups are considering the same subjects or themes as those covered in the morning's sermon, this may be especially effective. Moran notes that "preaching to the unconverted can be both ineffective and offensive."[206] He is suggesting that only those for whom the community's text are meaningful may benefit from the explication of that text.

In all of these forms of discourse, talking together face-to-face adds a dimension that is lacking in electronic communication.

Chapter Thirteen

The Centers Approach to Learning

"Well designed centers ... are a key way the teacher can
make student-centered, hands-on learning come alive."
—Harvey Daniels and Marilyn Bizar

Most writing about the centers approach to teaching and learning
is focused on secular education, and not many religious education
curriculum resources suggest that time for centers be built into class
time. The forty-five-minute or one hour session may not seem long
enough to have centers or other optional activities, but breaking the
time into fifteen or twenty minute segments makes it possible to shift
from one form of teaching to another. The teacher for children and
youth will not ordinarily need more than ten or twenty minutes for
presentation or "direct teaching," depending on the age of those in
the group. (The sermon adults hear during class time is usually about
twenty minutes long.) Centers, conferencing, and a wide variety of
activities may be a productive use of the remainder of the time the
group has together.

"A learning center is a small area within the classroom where
students work alone or interact with others, using instructional
materials to explore one or more subject areas," says Michael Opitz

in his book about learning centers.[207] "It is a place where a variety of activities introduce, reinforce, add/or extend learning, often without the assistance of the classroom teacher."

Key concepts that are required to make learning centers "worthwhile and genuine" are, according to Daniels and Bizar: something to learn or discover (not merely reviewing prior learning), some kind of interaction (talking and working together in small groups), and a tangible outcome, such as notes in a journal, solutions to a puzzle, or something similar. Some centers will be equipped with something for the participant to take away, such as a trinket, a small toy, or a sticker related to the theme of the center. Some may require students to leave something, as well—a response to a question, a completed crossword puzzle, a reflection. In order for students to participate without the teacher's direct involvement, posted instructions must be clear and understandable.[208] Not all centers need to be planned for small groups; there is great value in having solo centers for children who want (or need) to work alone. Learning centers should not be routine worksheets or coloring "within the lines," but feature real opportunities for interesting work, such as writing, drawing, or another creative project.

Activity centers may be simpler, with instructions given in pictures. Some may not need instructions, such as block corner, housekeeping corner, plant center, or painting corner set up with several easels and easily accessed paints. Painting should be done near the sink, if there is one in the room. The housekeeping corner, book corner, and block corner are staples in early childhood classrooms. Free play in religious education programs for young children may take advantage of these centers. Others that focus more directly on curriculum goals may be added. Activity centers are especially good for younger children or some children with special needs. Centers may be as simple as a bulletin board with materials that will be of interest to the group.

Decentralizing the Classroom

Ironically, centers decentralize the classroom, permitting teachers to work individually with children who need special attention or who have been absent and may need help catching up with the flow of the class. Centers are especially good for those who miss classes, giving them an opportunity to independently interact with the activities from missed sessions.

Centers or stations provide opportunities for individualized learning, giving the learner an opportunity to work at his or her own pace, as well as inspiring cooperative learning when students are able to work together on projects. They provide opportunities for children to revisit favorite activities, such as reading the same book over and over again, listening to a favorite song (with earphones), working on the same jigsaw puzzle week after week, or constructing more and more houses for a planned community. Giving active children optional learning activities for part of the session decreases the likelihood of boredom and misbehavior.

"Decentralizing the class also avoids discipline problems by helping to create a warm, friendly environment, one which is not conducive to conflict and tension," says Kim Marshall, middle school teacher and author of a book on the use of learning stations.[209]

The mixed age classroom setting is a natural place to use centers. Children of different ages and abilities may work together, helping one another as needed. The older child may read instructions aloud to younger ones and show them how to use materials.

Well planned centers offer activities that mesh with a variety of learning styles or intelligences and permit children to learn in ways that interest them. In week day school children may be required to visit all centers, but in religious education groupings that isn't necessary, even when desirable. The use of centers gives teachers an opportunity to exercise their own creativity. "There's tremendous artistry—and lots of teacherly sweat equity—in the design of centers that both embody concepts and support kid-run inquiry," say Daniels and Bizar.[210] Volunteer teachers may wish to enlist others to help with centers. A teacher education program might feature creating learning centers for individual classrooms by teaching teams.

Armstrong recommends that centers be geared to the eight intelligences. These are only a few of his examples, all of which are appropriate in faith development classrooms:

- Linguistic—book-nook or library area
- Logical-mathematical—science center
- Spatial—art area
- Bodily-kinesthetic—open space for creative movement
- Musical—music or listening lab (with different sounds to listen to)
- Interpersonal—round table for group discussion
- Intrapersonal—study carrels or a loft
- Natural—plant center with tools and supplies.[211]

Types of Centers

Centers are generally built around the theme of the curriculum, although there are generic ones suitable for any classroom, such as the previously mentioned book corners, plant centers, listening stations, food preparation centers, card making centers, and others. Each new season brings opportunities for new centers with seasonal themes. A center with a board game provides an opportunity for several children to play together.

Attendance centers may give children an opportunity to mark themselves present (perhaps by placing a designated sticker on an individual folder or a common wall chart), pick up name tags and cushions to sit on, as well as any other materials the teacher would like them to have to begin the session. Visitors or newcomers may find materials for making name tags at this center.

Record some of the activities in the classroom throughout the year, using a digital camera and computer, to make a DVD slideshow for a viewing center. Young children especially enjoy watching such compilations over and over again. Music or stories related to the theme of the class may be recorded and listened to by one child with earphones or by a small group using a speaker.

Activities designed for individuals or small groups in any curriculum may be adapted for use as centers in future sessions. Projects from one session may be available in centers format later on for children who were absent on the day they were done in class, or for children who like to repeat activities.

The meeting room may feature permanent centers with changing topics and activities, and/or rotating temporary centers. While it is true centers take up space, they don't have to take huge amounts. Most classrooms have four corners that can be used as centers, and a moveable table in the middle of the room may serve as a craft center but be taken away for circle time, whole group meetings, or active games. An art cart with basic craft materials can be present every Sunday or moved from room to room on a rotating basis. Bulletin boards, boxes, tubs, and dishpans may be utilized in centers, especially if materials need to be moved into and out of the classroom each Sunday. They may also be used as learning boxes, as discussed in chapter two. Folded cardboard or screens make a center when learning materials are affixed, ideally with a small table and chairs nearby. Two children in one class made their own work area by placing two chairs back to back and kneeling opposite each other to work with materials placed on the chair seats.[212] If space is really limited, centers materials may be placed on a table and children may take them to an area of the room where they are comfortable working, as is done with learning boxes in Godly Play.

Any teacher using centers (especially if children are not familiar with them) needs to think ahead about management of centers, especially scheduling them if spontaneous choice isn't working. This can be done by issuing tickets or counting off. It's okay to assign them, if children have a hard time deciding what they want to do.

Several centers on the same subject provide an opportunity for learners to explore the subject in more depth. This can be problematic when space is limited. Opitz gives examples of four centers on the same topic, with instructions for all four on the same poster.[213] One can imagine that the materials for all of the activities are below the poster. His topics happen to be teeth, eggs, and friendship, but any topic would do. For example, a poster with instructions for four centers on "Our Church" might have materials for the four in numbered boxes or baskets below the poster. One might have writing materials with the instruction to "write, or tell someone, about your first day at this church." Another might say "Draw a picture of our church or draw a picture of what you think our church should look like. Place your picture on the bulletin board if you wish." Yet another might include a jigsaw puzzle made from a picture of the church. The fourth might say something like "Our church name is _____. We are Unitarian Universalists. We like to sing, talk, work, and play together. Leave a picture or just write on one of the cards in the basket below telling about one thing you like to do at church. Take a bookmark with our principles from the basket below."

Centers are more commonly used with young children than with older ones. They are almost never used with teens, although there is no good reason that they are not. Classrooms for youth may already be more spatially flexible and casual than children's spaces, making it easy to set up some centers. These may be teacher made or the youth may make them. In a program where all ages are using the same theme, youth may enjoy making centers for younger children. But centers are not necessarily for the young only; I have used them with some success in a theological school classroom, in teacher education programs, and in a women's spirituality class. The iconic multimedia curriculum *The Haunting House* made use of a variety of centers, including "our regular interest centers: clay, carpentry, books, blocks, puzzles, step ladder, sleeping, and records."[214] Among the other centers was a conversation center, where a teacher was stationed and children could come and go as they wished. "Through conversation [children] are often able to sort out their feelings and thoughts, identify and clarify them, and therefore know themselves more deeply."[215]

Other examples of activity and learning centers in Unitarian Universalist curriculum materials may be found in *Celebrating Our Roots and Branches,*[216] *Special Times,*[217] and *A World of New Friends,* a thirteen week program that uses centers in each session.[218] Religious educators have adapted many activities from Tapestry of Faith programs to create centers.

Chapter Fourteen

Real World Experiences

The impact of the real world, experienced firsthand,
is unmatched by any book, movie or slide show—
we should all be field trip enthusiasts.
—Kim Marshall

Real world experiences are those that take learners out of the classroom and into the world or that bring experiences from life outside the classroom into that space. Harvey Daniels and Marilyn Bizar introduce the concept this way in their book *Methods That Matter*: "Authentic experiences in schools can be as small as writing a real letter to ask for an autographed picture, and as large as school wide projects like planting a garden, setting up a recycling center, or investigating the sources of pollution on a local river. Just as in real life, these experiences are inherently messy; problems need to be identified, complexity needs to be faced, and solutions must be found."[219]

Subjects that appeal to the interest and natural curiosity of children can be utilized in the religious education program. If teachers are alert to ideas the children bring forth, and if the program is flexible enough for them to take advantage of it, many relevant, meaningful activities will enliven the program. A story may prompt a child to suggest a trip to a farm, a park, or a public building of interest, or encourage another to suggest preparing a meal for their parents. Older children may bring an awareness of a local environmental issue warranting study and possible action.

As with all other learning activities, real world experiences call for reflection. Asking participants to write "what I learned on the field trip" will not be as productive as ongoing conversations, art responses, and incorporating such learning into future planning.

Classroom Activities

Any number of activities can bring the outside world into the classroom. Among them are cooking and baking. For the youngest children, preparing pretend meals in the housekeeping corner is a favorite activity. As they grow older they can participate in all sorts of food experiences: growing, harvesting, preparing, cooking, and eating. Food preparation may be related to a curriculum theme, such as making applesauce during a unit on Johnny Appleseed. Making Stone Soup is a favorite activity, playing on the folk tale of a traveler who puts stones into a soup pot of water and then coaxes the villagers to add meat and vegetables to the mix. Each child or family may bring a potato, or a carrot, or some other vegetable. Class time may not be long enough to cook meat thoroughly, and as many families are vegetarian, it is best to leave it out. Cookies may be baked for a special celebration, or to send to a homeless shelter or to a family that has suffered a loss.

Sewing, quilting, and other forms of needlework can be done by older children, teens, and adults. Even young children can contribute to a quilt by drawing pictures or signing their names on fabric. These can be gifts for anyone for whom it would be useful. I was once the recipient of such a gift. The summer before I went away to college our house burned to the ground. About a month later I received a handmade quilt from the small Union Methodist Church in Rye,

Arkansas, where I had led a Youth Activities Week earlier that year. It is tattered and torn but I still have it.

Banners or hangings for the classroom, hallways, or to carry in a processional for a special service can be made in the classroom, using felt, fabric, glue, and other materials. Examples are peace banners for Memorial Day, welcome banners for the installation of a new minister, or theme-related banners for a congregational anniversary celebration. Posters, fliers, or signs may be made, perhaps advertising social service or social justice projects or to carry in a protest march or demonstration.

Exploring family religious histories or the congregation's history are real world activities that begin in the classroom but lead to research in the home or the church community. Oral interviews, family trees, timelines, scrapbooks, photographs, and videos are some of the tools to use in these endeavors.

Gardening

Experiencing the miracle of growth through gardening, on a small or large scale, indoors or out, is satisfying for people of all ages. Any room with a sunny exposure can be home to plants. If there is no sunny exposure, it might be worth keeping plants elsewhere during the week and bringing them in, perhaps on a rolling cart, for group time.

Fortunate groups will be able to grow things outside. Planting vegetables in a community garden, harvesting them, and helping to distribute them is a long-term project that involves a variety of activities.

Group Investigations

A group investigation of a topic gives members of the group responsibility for learning about the topic and sharing their information with the others. The whole group discusses a subject, responds to it, and then breaks it down into smaller parts to be researched by small groups. Each group then investigates the assigned area.

This is useful for building community and is especially good for social justice projects, giving students (older children, teens, and adults) needed information to make good decisions before taking action. It may be used for a variety of areas of interest.

Theological students used this method to acquaint themselves with Tapestry of Faith, the UUA's online religious education curriculum. Each small group studied materials for a different age group and then presented their findings and an activity from one curriculum to the class. They were asked to identify teaching methods and learning activities, to consider appropriateness for the age group designed for, adaptability, how each program meshes with Unitarian Universalist values and principles, and to examine them through an Anti-Racist Anti-Oppression lens. Through this investigation they learned about the current curriculum in use in most congregations. They really liked the stories and began using them immediately in worship services and classes.

Another seminary class studied proposals for changes to UUA governance as their group investigation.

Field Trips

Because signed permission slips are necessary for minors going on field tips without a parent or guardian, they should be planned well ahead of time and well publicized in order to be sure that all who wish to participate are able to. Even so, there are often visitors or even regular attendees who missed the announcement and show up to find they are missing the trip. Better yet, plan to take most trips outside of the Sunday morning time frame. Groups then become multigenerational, with parents responsible for their own children, doing away with the need for permission slips. There should, however, be a list of names of all participating with the leader of the trip and a copy at the church with a designated person.

Visits to museums may focus on items related to curriculum materials. They are appropriate for art appreciation, general interest in the focus of the museum, or to see some specific thing that has been the subject of interest in the program. Years ago classes studying Akhenaten visited the King Tut exhibit at the Smithsonian in Washington, DC.

Appropriate movies, musical performances, and stage productions are especially good for multigenerational groups. If there is a possibility that ethical issues may be involved, plan for thoughtful discussion before deciding to make the trip. Children studying about Universalism and preparing for a play about showman P.T. Barnum went to the circus, creating concern among members of the congregation. In this case, the issue was animal cruelty. Some have issues with zoos also.

Visits to a senior center give children an opportunity to interact with older people and to perform a service by bringing their presence to the group. They may wish to sing a song or to take cards for the elders.

Middle school and sometimes high school groups studying other religions often visit other places of worship. These should be planned and prepared for carefully for optimum value. Visiting other Unitarian Universalist congregations can be a learning experience, too. All of these work well as multigenerational activities. Many congregations plan visits to Partner Churches in Europe or India, some on a yearly basis. International trips will probably be for teens and adults only.

Youth conferences and district and regional assemblies or the annual UUA General Assembly provide opportunities for learning about Unitarian Universalism on different levels.

Many congregational groups visit Boston on Unitarian Universalist Heritage Tours, but such tours are appropriate anywhere there are a sufficient number of Unitarian Universalist sites or places with artifacts related to Unitarian Universalism. Many cities have several congregations and most meeting places are different enough that a tour of even three indicates the variety of buildings and the congregations that meet within them.

The statue of Thomas Starr King in the national Capitol building was a favorite stop on UU Heritage Tours in Washington, DC, until it was replaced by one of Ronald Reagan. The King statue may now be seen in a garden outside the California state Capitol building in Sacramento. There is another in Golden Gate Park in San Francisco. There are places of Unitarian Universalist significance in most regions of the country. Before making firm plans, check with people in the area you plan to visit to get optimal information. Middle school or high school groups will want to meet with others their age in the cities they visit.

Experiences With Nature

Nature walks, camping trips, stargazing, bird watching, and visits to planetariums, nature centers, and nature preserves provide opportunities for many different kinds of experiences, depending on interest and age of the group and how knowledgeable leadership is. Picking berries, apples, or pumpkins by large or small groups are popular seasonal activities. Produce may be taken home to eat, prepared for a church supper, or shared with a food bank or shelter.

Congregational retreats give families a chance to work together at cooking, washing dishes, and cleaning up in a spirit of shared responsibility with other families and individuals. Retreats and camping offer opportunities for play, hiking, and group singing.

A church I served planned a camping trip; we borrowed a tent, packed the car, and anticipated a most enjoyable weekend. We set up the tent and, after a picnic supper and singing by the campfire, settled down for sleep. About midnight rain came down in torrents, totally flooding the tent. The four of us and our very wet dog (happily a small one) spent the rest of the night in a Volkswagen

Beetle, thinking the event was a total washout. This story has a happy ending, as the sun came out and things dried out quickly. Things can go wrong on trips, however, so it is good to have plans for alternate activities.

Service to Congregation and Community

Religious education groups often provide service to the congregation beyond helping with worship services. These may be helping with building or grounds maintenance or playground construction, painting (plain walls or murals), planting a garden, or working in a greenhouse on the grounds. Older children and teens can assist with many of these projects. Teen groups often have bake sales or car washes or offer their services to do odd jobs to raise money for a special project as well as providing a service to the community.

Congregations and classes can participate in social service and social justice projects in many ways. Among these are: cleaning up streams and shallow waterways, recycling projects, or putting together toiletry bags or preparing food for homeless shelters. Whatever the project, it is a good idea to learn in advance what is needed. When one congregation prepared dinner for a homeless shelter, two youth spent an afternoon creating forty elaborate individual salads, only to learn that the intended recipients really preferred simpler, perhaps more familiar, food. For holiday projects, each child or family may bring a food item to take to a food bank or to put together boxes for Thanksgiving or Christmas dinners.

One group of children decorated and filled shoe boxes for children who were at a women's shelter with their mothers. Combs, small toys, notepads, and pencils were among the items included. Leaders learned how many children were at the shelter that weekend, so freshly baked cookies could be added to boxes for those children.

Mission or service learning trips and work camps for teens and adults may take them to parts far and wide. Some of these projects include building or repairing houses or work in the community, with more person to person activities. Take time to gather needed information and plan ahead for a successful experience.

Almost all of the "Faith in Action" components of Tapestry of Faith include some kind of real world experience: service to the congregation, service to the community, field trips, and so on. "Taking it Home" components have suggestions for families to engage in authentic experiences together.

One religious educator reports all of these Real World Experiences from the congregation she serves: field trips (including one to the local cemetery), social justice activities, group investigations, cooking, travel to Budapest and Transylvania, Thanksgiving boxes, sandwich and sock distribution after a youth sleepover, and cooking in a summer program.[220]

Chapter Fifteen

Reflection and Meditation

"Too often religious education is so goal-
oriented and curriculum-conscious
that it loses sight of its mission to minister
to the religious life of the child."
—Mark Searle

The seventh method proposed for appropriate religious education is that of reflection and/or meditation. Opportunities may be given for spiritual practices at every age level, although of course they need to be designed appropriately. Some of the specific activities in this category are coloring mandalas, guided imagery or meditation, making and using prayer or meditation beads, creating personal altars, making prayer flags, using labyrinths, rock balancing, body prayers, and dance or movement.

Centering

A few centering moments to begin the group time together or for a closing activity is appropriate for all age groups. Gather everyone into the circle. It is preferable to have everyone sitting on the floor when it is possible for all in the group and there is some kind of floor covering. If seated on the floor, legs should be crossed in front of participants, back straight, hands in the lap, palms up, and eyes closed—if only for the briefest of times. Say something like, "Let's breathe quietly together … Take a deep breath, drawing the air in through your nose, and letting it out quietly through your mouth … Again … one more nice quiet breath … Now may we feel centered as we begin our circle time …"

Mindfulness and Meditation

For longer times of meditation you may wish to have dim lighting (perhaps candlelight) and quiet music to set the mood. Scented candles, incense or other aromatics may trigger allergies, so be aware of any known allergies before using scents.

One simple mindfulness meditation, usually attributed to Dr. Jon Kabat-Zinn, is the Raisin Meditation. Many variations may be found online, or you can craft your own. For this you will need one raisin for each participant and less than five minutes.

Hand one raisin to each person. Say something like:

Hold the raisin in your hand, or between a finger and thumb. Imagine you have never seen a raisin before. Look at the raisin. Really look at it. See the different folds and ridges and how the light reflects off them as you turn it in your hand. Turn the raisin over and feel the texture. Close your eyes and just feel the raisin. Now, open your eyes and hold the raisin beneath your nose. Can you smell the raisin? Focus on the odor. Now bring the raisin to your lips and place it in your mouth. Don't eat it yet, just notice having it in your mouth…. Chew the raisin but don't swallow it just yet…. When you feel ready, swallow the raisin.

This is one way to encourage children (and others) to be mindful and appreciate all aspects of eating and other activities of everyday life.

Guided Imagery

Another form of meditation is guided imagery. Older children might enjoy one like this, for Earth Day or any lesson on the environment:

Spaceship Meditation

Imagine that you are in a spaceship.… You are going on a trip to outer space but you know that you will return.… You feel safe but at the same time adventurous. Imagine that the spaceship takes off and you are thrust way, way up in the sky.… As you begin to orbit the earth, you realize that you can see it … that beautiful blue-green ball, seeming so small and fragile.… As you look at the earth imagine that you are thinking of how much it needs our help and care.… Now you know it is time for the return trip.… Where will your spaceship splash down? Perhaps far from land in the Pacific Ocean … Imagine that you are hurtling through space, back down into the waters of this beautiful planet.… Now prepare for the landing, knowing that you will be coming back into this room, with this group … And, here we are … you may want to open your eyes and look around you.… Now, let's talk about what we can do, separately or together, to help our fragile earth to heal.

Mandalas

The word *mandala* comes from the Sanskrit word for circle. It is a spiritual and ritual symbol in Hinduism and Buddhism and is used as a spiritual tool in various traditions. One may meditate on a completed mandala—a picture or one made of colored sand— or for more personal involvement may draw, paint, or color one's own. Many designs are available in booklets and online. Even small children may find that coloring mandalas is calming and a way of focusing attention. Many commercially available ones have detailing too fine for little fingers, so be sure to have appropriate designs for younger children. Colored markers work well in most cases.

For formal meditation on a mandala, one first sets an intention for the meditation, such as more clearly understanding some aspect of one's spiritual journey or seeking guidance, and then focuses on the mandala. Less formally, one may just enjoy the process.

Beads

Individuals may appreciate creating and using beads for expressing gratitude or for meditation or prayer. Prayer beads are used in many religious traditions, including Hinduism, Buddhism, Islam, Sikhism, the Baha'i Faith, and Christianity, to mark the repetitions of prayers, chants, or devotions. Many children may be familiar with Catholic rosary beads. The exact origins of prayer beads are uncertain, but they are an ancient tradition. They may be used for meditation and reflection, as well as counting prayers or chants.

When making a necklace or bracelet for this purpose each bead may be selected to represent an intention, a person, a reading or any thing the person wishes to meditate on while fingering that particular bead.

RoyGBiv is the name given to the colors of the rainbow to remember the order of the colors: red, orange, yellow, green, blue, indigo, and violet. In Unitarian Universalism, rainbow beads are used, with each color representing one of the seven principles affirmed by congregations. Many variations of the principles have been formulated to make them clearer to children; any of these may be used with the colored beads. One such variation matches the first letter of each principle with the first letter of the corresponding color:

- Red—Respect all beings.
- Orange—Offer fair and kind treatment to all.
- Yellow—Yearn to learn.
- Green—Grow together.

- Blue—Believe in your ideas and act on them.
- Indigo—Insist on peace, freedom, and justice for all.
- Violet—Value our interdependence with nature.[221]

The concept is for children to reflect on each of the principles as they finger the particular bead representing it.

Altars for Classroom or Home

Groups may want to create an altar, or worship setting, for use at Circle Time. You might start with a chalice and add other items as you go along, perhaps a stone related to a story, or a leaf picked up on a nature walk. Older children might want to make personal altars to take home. The personal altar, shrine, or treasure shelf is a set-aside sacred space for special objects, such as pictures, flowers, shells, or stones to help the individual focus on life's blessings and to honor the holy. If planning to have children make altars, devote a session to considering what each child might want to include to create an atmosphere of quiet for centering and meditation.

Labyrinths

The ancient labyrinth, used for walking meditation, is symbolic of wholeness. The design combines the imagery of the circle and the spiral into a meandering, but purposeful, path to the center, and then back out. This traditional spiritual pathway has had a resurgence in recent years and many congregations have their own labyrinth, either outdoors or painted on canvas to be laid out on the floor on occasion. These are usually walked without shoes, indoors, and the meditative quality of the experience is enhanced by quiet music. These are not mazes; there is only one way to the center and it leads back out. There are no walls and no one can get lost.

Many small versions, called finger labyrinths or desk labyrinths, are available as portable spiritual aids. They are made of Lucite, wood, bamboo, pewter, or other materials. There are versions online that may be downloaded and printed.[222]

Rock Balancing

Rock balancing—when rocks are the right size and shape—can be a meaningful activity for all ages. This works well for families or small multigenerational groups. Some time should be taken before the activity to talk about the importance of working quietly and, in a group, cooperatively. I was delighted to discover balanced rocks on a visit to the Thomas Jefferson Memorial Church in Charlottesville, Virginia, where a rock pile for this purpose was located at the base of a large tree on their grounds. Note that rock balancing is not the building of cairns as a memorial or to signify that an event has taken place. It is the practice of lifting and placing somewhat heavy rocks one atop the other so that they balance without adhesive or glue of any kind. Although it is now gaining favor as an art form or hobby, this is an ancient spiritual practice.

Body Prayer

Embodied prayer—whether seated, standing, or moving about—may be more comfortable for many Unitarian Universalists than spoken prayer. Using the hands, sitting or standing in an intentional way, leisurely walking, walking in meditation, or forming yoga poses may be meaningful for people of all ages. Any of these may be performed in silence or accompanied by meditative music. When organizing children in any form of body prayer, be sure each one has sufficient space to keep from bumping into one another. This simple body prayer might be used as a ritual part of the Sunday morning gathering:

> As we stand in a circle, look toward the center of the circle, so we can see one another's faces. Stretch out your arms gently and make sure we have enough space to stand without

touching one another. Let's move back a little to make the circle just a little larger. Okay, everybody stand as quietly as you can, and breathe in, breathe out.... Now, close your eyes gently, not too tightly.... Put your hands out in front of you, palms up.... Let's say together, "I welcome the morning"....

And then "'I welcome the day"'.... Reach your hands out to your sides, towards those next to you in the circle. Let's say together, "I feel your presence".... And now, as you open your eyes, say, "I open my eyes. I see your faces." Let's join hands and say "I join hands with you in the spirit of love" and move toward the center of the circle. Let's say together "May our group be blessed." You may drop your hands, and let's take our places.

Dances of the Universal Peace

This form of sacred dance is a group spiritual practice which works well with multigenerational groups, but may be used with others, as well. This is another form of body prayer. These simple circle dances are intended to cultivate inner peace and harmony. They are taught by a dance leader and most are easy to learn. Samuel Lewis, credited with being the originator of these dances, studied with a Sufi teacher and the dances were originally called Sufi dances. They are not, however, exclusively Islamic. They honor the universality found in world religions.[223]

Reflective Assessment

We don't hand out grades in faith development programs, nor should we, but some reflective assessment, preferably self-assessment is appropriate. This may be done in group conversation, asking such questions as "What have we learned about _____ in our group?" and/or "What more would we like to know, or to do, before the end of the year (or month)?" If class time ordinarily includes time for centers or options, plan to have conferences with each learner during that time, over a period of weeks. One teacher may continue to relate to those participating in other activities while another conducts the conference. Even young children can express their feelings, learnings, and concerns in a reflective conference. Keeping a portfolio of student work provides a focus for conferences with older children. Family conferences are a good idea, too, but it is often hard to arrange these.

Tapestry of Faith

Tapestry of Faith programs are rich with reflective and meditative practices. The website notes "We appreciate the value of spiritual practice as a means of deepening faith and integrating beliefs and values with everyday life."[224] The labyrinth is central to *Creating Home.*[225] Prayer and meditation are included in Session Four of *Signs of Our Faith.* Samples are provided for families to read together at home with suggestions that they choose one to use regularly as a family ritual.[226] One session of *Moral Tales*[227] has instructions for children to make prayer bead necklaces or bracelets for their own use. Circle times, the "Criss-Cross-Applesauce" position for meditation, and other practices are found throughout.

Chapter Sixteen

Tomorrow's Children and Today's Heritage

"The depths of human experience are emotional, and vital
religion will always fathom these depths.—Sophia Lyon Fahs

My vision for the future of religious education in Unitarian
Universalism calls for a radical re-imagining of what we offer to
children on Sunday mornings. I'd like to see "the Sunday morning
hour" be welcoming to all children and youth without regard to
registration, family commitment, or attendance patterns, to be more
like worship than school, yet to be based on a sound pedagogy and
offer both lively and reflective activities. The morning's experience
should be open to all, welcoming and inclusive.

Children should be welcomed in the same way that adults
are, free to come for one event or to stay on forever, welcome to
participate without a financial investment (although one is usually
required for membership.) Frequent visitors who consider themselves
part of the community are not at all uncommon, but registration
fees, class lists, and attendance records are a barrier to children doing
the same, in many congregations.

Our Sunday morning programs for children were designed for a different era, a less mobile one, with more clearly defined denominational affiliations, fewer visitors in our congregations, and not so many families with children who can attend every other Sunday at most. These programs reflect their origins in the Sunday School, being organized into classes, often closely graded. They reflect, too, the era of the "School of Religion." For the most part our programs have not kept pace with more contemporary understandings of education for faith development.

The prevailing concept of programming is based on an understanding of religious education programs as exclusive to those children who have been enrolled by their parents, often by paying a fee, and sometimes—but not always—open to visitors. Visitors may be asked to sign up/pay up within a certain period of time if they wish to continue coming. Usually the plans are for sequential learning, and the assumption is that every child who comes will have experienced the same lessons as every other child, so little effort is expended to make each session holistic and sufficient unto itself. Some programs (notably Our Whole Lives or Coming of Age) are closed to newcomers or visitors, even when it is the only option provided for that particular age group.

I once found a sixth grade girl wandering the halls of a large church, visiting with a friend but denied admission to the classroom, although it was not intended to be a closed class. In another church one morning in late winter, I met with a family who came hoping to join and participate, only to learn that there would be no class for their seventh grader until the next fall, as it was too late for him to enter the closed class in progress. They found another congregation.

This is not to say that children should just be brought and turned loose, without being properly identified or supervised. Clearly there is a need to know who they are and what responsible adult has brought them to church. Teachers need to know if children have allergies or difficulties that might be triggered by anything in the morning program, such as food, activities, or craft materials.

Visitor cards are to be required of all—with appropriate information concerning the child's name and age, allergies, special needs, and the name of a responsible adult. All children (and youth) could wear name tags with such information on the back. I am not suggesting that we don't have a list of regular attendees, just that the program should be designed to actively welcome others.

This flexibility need not preclude the maintenance of a substantive program, although it might be of a different kind. Current groupings could be maintained if desired. Except in large churches, groupings might need to serve a wider age range. Small congregations might have one large group, plus child care for the very youngest, while mid-size congregations might have three or four groupings, sorted either by age or interest.

Rich possibilities for content will emerge. It will be easier to respond with a Sunday morning session devoted to a current issue or congregational celebration, as each weekly unit is designed to stand alone. Programs may be organized around themes, in "pillars" or "rotation of themes," and use any and all of the methods recommended in this book.

Family Designed Learning

As most religious growth and learning takes place in the family, we should provide more resources for parents. Some already in use in many congregations include: parent education programs, multigenerational activities, "take homes" from Sunday morning experiences, and a more focused role for parents in determining what educational opportunities the congregation may provide for their children.

The possibilities for individualized learning plans or family designed learning have not been explored to any great extent among us. A combination of internet/computer learning, family reading and discovery, and participation in workshops, classes, and groups as outlined above might be utilized.

Learning goals for individual children and youth would be set in a conference with child, parent, and congregational representative (a professional or volunteer trained for such activity). Even very young children have definite ideas about what they like to do and want to learn.

Instituting such a process could be time consuming, but once it is in place, new families could be invited to participate in the process as soon as they have indicated an interest in being more involved and engaged in the congregation. They may then indicate that they wish to nurture their child's spiritual development and provide opportunities for religious growth and learning outside of the Sunday morning hour. Beginning such a program would not require every child to have a plan in place on the first day of any given year, but could be done over a period of weeks, or even months, while activities were ongoing.

Not Sunday Morning Only

A structure with more flexibility on Sunday morning, plus outside avenues for learning, would provide enrichment to all of our programs. Even though all parents usually are invited to participate in planning, no one program can satisfy the desires of all parents or meet the needs of all children. But religious education staff (professional and volunteer) can work with families to help design other learning opportunities: workshops, after school or summer programs focusing on specific topics (Unitarian Universalist identity, Jewish heritage, Christian heritage), and the continuation of special programs such as Our Whole Lives (OWL) and Coming of Age (COA). Multigenerational events, such as family retreats, camping, museum trips, camps and conferences, can offer many opportunities for learning.

Such a Sunday morning structure would not require more adult leadership than traditional programs, and might require less. Volunteer leaders for groups at other times would be needed, although religious professionals should play a large role in these activities. Ministers often bemoan the difficulty in being engaged with children due to classes conflicting with the Sunday morning worship hour; this kind of scheduling would obviate that problem. Some people who don't want to commit to long-term Sunday morning teaching would be willing to lead an occasional workshop or field trip.

Some congregations might move toward more multigenerational groupings on Sunday morning. Others will wish to continue having loosely graded programs for children and youth. Either may be accommodated in the Worship-Education model, with all gathering for worship, then separating for activities, and all returning for the closing worship.

Opportunities should be provided for classes, workshops, field trips, at times other than the "Sunday morning hour." Even in small congregations this is workable. For example, a "girls group" composed of six or eight girls ages six to twelve, or twelve to fourteen, could get together at a time convenient for them and their parents, and explore issues and concerns together. Boys' groups could do the same. Clubs—book clubs, computer clubs, etc.—could provide occasions for study, friendship, and reflection. Workshops, classes, and groups organized at other times (before or after this hour, weekdays, summertime) could provide more focused learning opportunities as deemed important by parents and the congregation. Registration for such groups would be appropriate. COA and OWL classes are sometimes offered at times other than Sunday morning and in my opinion this is preferable.

Plans of course would need to be reconsidered and updated from time to time. Individual needs and wishes would be considered in planning optional activities and events to offer. For example, if several children want to learn more about the Bible, or if their parents want them to, workshops or classes could be tailored to the age and developmental levels of those who have already indicated an interest, and others would be invited to participate as well.

In addition to re-imagining the way we see Sunday morning, it calls for the creation of slightly different materials than we normally use, although many in use now could be adapted. To organize ourselves differently for Sunday morning, we can look at such programs as Rotation and Way Cool Sunday School, although with the intention of seeing them as one component of the religious education/faith development program, rather than the only one. Montessori-inspired programs, including but not limited to Godly Play and Spirit Play, and the use of Small Group Ministry models may offer inspiration for making the Sunday morning hour more a time of spiritual nurture than schooling. Learning centers on principles and sources could be available from time to time. When congregations use theme-based ministry, Sunday morning groups may consider these themes, and they may be used for ongoing learning centers.

The Educating Community

As we seek to become more truly educating communities, instead of dividing the church into worship, education, music, service, and social action components, perhaps we may think of ways in which we can provide all of these experiences to people of all ages.

Social media and interactive computer learning will no doubt play a more important role in our congregational life as time goes on. Innovations in technology offer new possibilities. Howard Gardner cautions that "Educators have always tinkered with promising technologies, and much of the history of education chronicles the varying fates of paper, books, lecture halls, filmstrips, television, computers, and other human artifacts. Current technologies seem tailor-made to help bring into reality the kind of 'MI approach' that I have endorsed…. Still, there are no guarantees. Many technologies have faded, and many others have been used superficially and unproductively…. That is why any consideration of education cannot

remain merely instrumental. Not merely computers, we must ask—
but computers for what? More broadly, education for what?"[228]

There is no doubt that social media, all week programming,
and religious education in the home will become more important
in the future. Nonetheless, there will always be times for gathering
together in religious community, in groups large and small, of
varying complements. We will always want to see one another's
faces, to hear one another's voices, to touch one another's hands.

We live in a time of change and uncertainty. We must be
courageous and creative to meet the needs of the times ahead. We
are called to new beginnings even as we honor what has gone before,
that we may be worthy of the heritage that we have been given. It is
our privilege and responsibility to contribute to this heritage of hope
and faith and love for today's children, and for tomorrow's.

Notes

Preface

[1] Dillard, *American Childhood*, 81.

Introduction

[2] Nieuwejaar, *The Gift of Faith*, 10.
[3] Palmer, *The Courage to Teach*, 10.
[4] Parker, *The Transient and Permanent in Christianity*, 118.
[5] O'Neal, Wesley, and Ford, *The Transient and Permanent in Liberal Religion*, 3.
[6] Fewkes, "Theodore Parker Speaks," in O'Neal, 42.
[7] Middleton, "How We Do What We Do in Religious Education" *Reader*, 34-47.
[8] Fahs, *Today's Children and Yesterday's Heritage*.

Chapter One. The Transient and Permanent in Religious Education

[9] Boys, *Educating in Faith: Maps & Visions*, 39.
[10] Ibid., 3.
[11] Ibid., 119.
[12] Moran, *Religious Education as a Second Language*, 7.
[13] Strong, "Synopsis of Unitarian Universalist Religious Education Eras," 1.
[14] Strong, *The Larger Message*, 35.

[15]   Murray, *A Universalist Catechism*. Lost to public view for many years, the catechism was republished by the Judith Sargent Murray Society in 1999, with an introduction by Bonnie Hurd Smith.

[16]   Navias, "A Short History of Unitarian Universalist Religious Education," *Reader. Graduate Level Course in Religious Education*, 3.

[17]   Strong, in a lecture "The Rise of the Sunday School Movement," at Murray Grove in 2014, 5.

[18]   Parke, *The Children Were My Teachers*, 49.

[19]   Fahs, *Today's Children and Yesterday's Heritage*, 16.

[20]   MacLean, *The Method is the Message*.

[21]   Commission III, Education and Liberal Religion, 50.

[22]   *Ibid.*, 51.

[23]   *Ibid.*, 56.

[24]   *Ibid.*, 61.

[25]   Robertson, "The Fahs/MacLean Era," 40.

[26]   *Ibid.*, 40.

[27]   *Ibid.*, 41.

[28]   Commission III, 58.

[29]   Hollerorth, H., "Focus on a New Era: The Making of a Curriculum," *The Register-Leader of the Unitarian Universalist Association* Volume 149 Number 4. April, 1967, 11.

[30]   Baker, *Retrospect*, 28.

[31]   Hollerorth, H., Editor, *Stone House Conversations*, 6.

[32]   *Report of the Religious Education Futures Committee*, 8.

[33]   Anastos and Marshak, editors, *Philosophy-Making for Unitarian Universalist Religious Growth and Learning*.

[34]   Gilbert and Nelson, *Religious Education and Social Action: Branches of the Same Tree*.

[35]   Essex Conversations Coordinating Committee, *Essex Conversations*, x.

[36]   www.uua.org/re/tapestry.

Chapter Two. Nurturing the Spirit

[37]   Carson, *The Sense of Wonder*, 42.

[38]   *Ibid.*, 52.

[39]   Robinson, *The Original Vision*, 11.

[40]   Nieuwejaar, *The Gift of Faith*, v.

[41]   Schulte, *Overwhelmed*, 10.

[42]   Miller, *The Spiritual Child*, 6.

43   *Ibid.*, 7.

44   Channing, *Discourse pronounced before to the Sunday-School Society, The Works of William E. Channing,* 448.

45   Simon and Harmin, "Subject Matter With a Focus on Values," 34.

46   Navias, "Checkpoints for Teachers," 2.

47   Neville, *Cultural and Community Roots of Liturgy,* 4.

48   Wolf, *Nurturing the Spirit in Non-Sectarian Classrooms, 13.*

49   *Ibid.*, 59.

50   *Ibid.*, 159.

51   *Ibid.*, 157.

52   Gilbert, *Growing Up Absorbed,* 151.

53   Searle, "Preface," *The Religious Potential of the Church,* 4.

Chapter Three. How We Learn: Theory

54   www.learning-theories.com

55   www.funderstanding.com

56   Jarvis, *Towards a Comprehensive Theory of Human Learning,* 5.

57   *Ibid.*, 199.

58   Illeris, *Contemporary Theories of Learning,* 7.

59   *Ibid.*, 12-14.

60   Elkjaer, *Pragmatism,* 75.

61   Jarvis, "Learning to be a Person in Society: Learning to be Me," 21-33.

62   Bruner, "Culture, Mind, and Education," 159-168.

63   Gardner, "Multiple Approaches to Understanding",108-109.

64   Moran, *Religious Education Development,* 146.

65   *Ibid.*, 147.

66   *Ibid.*, 149-152.

67   *Ibid.*, 153.

68   Gardner, *Intelligence Reframed,* 36-41.

69   *Ibid.*, 52.

70   *Ibid.*, 64-66.

71   Chapman, *If the Shoe Fits: How to Develop Multiple Intelligences in the Classroom.*

72   Armstrong, *Multiple Intelligences in the Classroom 3rd Edition,*109.

73   *Ibid.*, 149-160.

74   Gardner, "Multiple Approaches to Understanding," 108-109.

75   Joyce, *Models of Teaching,* 402.

76   Gardner, *Frames of Mind,* 89-91.

Chapter Four. How We Learn: Practice

77   Palmer, *The Courage to Teach,* 133.

78   *Ibid.,* 73. For more about the emotional space of the classroom see pages 74 through 82, where Parker discusses paradoxes of space.

79   Hurd, *Nurturing Children and Youth,* x.

80   Patton, *Welcoming Children With Special Needs,* 56.

81   *Ibid.,* p. 59.

82   Armstrong, *Multiple Intelligences in the Classroom.* Particular attention is paid to special needs students in Chapter 11 "MI Theory and Special Education," 149-160.

83   *Ibid.,* 150-151.

84   Berryman, *Teaching Godly Play,* 44-47.

85   www.lreda.org

86   Brandt, "On Teaching for Understanding," 7.

Chapter Five. How We Teach: Approaches

87   Freire, *A Pedagogy for the Oppressed,* 53.

88   Navias, "Two Contrasting Philosophies of Religious Education," 27.

89   *Ibid.,* 3.

90   *Ibid.,* 8.

91   *Ibid.,* 49.

92   Daniels and Bizar, *Methods That Matter,* 47.

93   *Ibid.,* 4.

94   *Ibid.,* 8.

95   Palmer, *The Courage to Teach,* 116.

96   *Ibid.,* 117.

97   *Ibid.,* 76.

98   Groome. *Christian Religious Education,* 137.

99   *Ibid.,* 207-208.

100 Moran, *Showing How. The Act of Teaching,* 38.

101 *Ibid.,* 39.

102 *Ibid.,* 3.

103 *Ibid.,* 90.

104 Ashton-Warner, *Teacher,* 35.

105 *Ibid.,* 1.

106 Nelson, "The Teacher as Spiritual Guide," 185.

107 Andrews, "The Soul Only Avails," 1.

108 Gutek, *The Montessori Method*, 42.

109 Wolf, *Nurturing the Spirit*, 5.

110 Berryman, *Godly Play*, 34-35.

111 www.spiritplay.com

112 Berryman, *Godly Play*, 17.

113 Penfold, *Spirit Play*, 15.

114 Hollerorth, H., "An Era of Change," 58.

115 *Ibid.*, 59.

116 Wiske, *Teaching for Understanding*, 4.

Chapter Six. How We Teach: Method

117 McLuhan, *Understanding Media*, *x*.

118 MacLean, *The Method is the Message*, 14.

119 Fahs, *Today's Children and Yesterday's Heritage*, 176.

120 Galindo, *The Craft of Christian Teaching*, 43.

121 Middleton, *Special Times*, 17-20.

122 Kimball, *Amazing Grace Field Test*, 1.

Chapter Seven. How We Organize: Models and Structures

123 Kent and Steward, *Learning by Heart*, 64.

124 Brandt, "Teaching for Understanding,"4.

125 Spoerl, *The Creative Process in Religious Education*, 42.

126 Stewart, Greg. "Sunday School is Dead—Long Live Sunday School." 274.

127 Armstrong-Hansche, and MacQueen. *Workshop Rotation*,

128 www.rotation/org.

129 O'Donnell and Dare. *Workshop Wonders*, 42-45

130 *Ibid.*, 82.

131 Henderson, "Worship and Sunday School: Which is best for your congregation?"

132 White, *Intergenerational Religious Education*, 50.

Chapter Eight. How We Organize: Groupings

133 Gutek, *The Montessori Method*, 14.

134 Bacharach, Hasslen, and Anderson. *Learning Together*, ix.

135 *Ibid.*, 2.

136   *Ibid.,* 21.

137   *Ibid.,* 9.

138   Ostrow, *A Room With a Different View,* 26.

139   *Ibid.,* 33.

140   *Ibid.,* 4.

141   Chase, Doan, and Contributing Educators. *Full Circle,* ix.

142   White, *Intergenerational Religious Education,*13.

143   Archer, "Outside the Box", 14-15.

144   Frediani, "Making Sure There is a There There", 56.

145   Henderson, "Worship and Sunday School: Which model is best for your congregation?," 5.

146   Griggs and Griggs, *Generations Learning Together,* 15.

147   *Ibid.,* 24.

148   White, 18.

149   *Ibid.,* 27.

150   *Ibid.,* 28.

Chapter Nine. Story, Stories, and Storytelling

151   Anderson and Foley. *Mighty Stories, Dangerous Rituals,* 13.

152   Crossan, *The Dark Interval* 1988, *42.*

153   *Ibid.,* 41.

154   Crossan, *The Dark Interval* 1975, 39-42.

155   *Ibid.,* 50.

156   *Ibid.,* 45.

157   Wesley, *Myths of Time and History,* 3.

158   Bumbaugh, *Unitarian Universalism,* 5.

159   Groome, *Christian Religious Education,* 205.

160   Palmer, *The Courage to Teach,* 76.

161   Hymnbook Resources Commission, *Singing the Living Tradition, x.*

162   Anderson and Foley, *Mighty Stories, Dangerous Rituals,* 3.

163   www.uua.org/re/tapestry.

164   Peebles, "Lessons from a Tube of Toothpaste" in *Windmills, Worship, and Wonder,* 2.

165   Crowley, *Windmills, Wonder, and Worship* and *Together Time.*

166   Harris, *Getting Started in Storytelling,* 21-24.

Chapter Ten. Creative Expression and the Development of Faith

[167] Kent and Steward, *Learning by Heart*, 5.
[168] Penfold, *Spirit Play*, 13.
[169] Tolley, *Child's Play*, 300-304.
[170] Berryman, *Godly Play*, 35.
[171] *Ibid.*, p. 35.
[172] Milgrom, *Handmade Midrash*, x.
[173] *Ibid.*, 6.
[174] *Ibid.*, 30.
[175] Blumberg, "President's Column," *REACH*, 1.
[176] Spoerl, *The Creative Process and Religious Education*, 31.
[177] *Ibid.*, 38.
[178] *Ibid.*, 42.
[179] Koch, *Wishes, Lies, and Dreams*, 1970.

Chapter Eleven. Learning Through Play

[180] Covey, *Chalice Children*.
[181] Armstrong, *Multiple Intelligences in the Classroom*, 107.
[182] Olson and York, *Creating Home*.
[183] United Nations Declaration of the Rights of the Child, 1.
[184] Kent and Steward, *Learning by Heart*, 162.
[185] www.nifplay.org.
[186] www.npr.org/blogs/ed/ 2014 *Why Adults Need Recess Too*.
[187] Davis, Haymaker, Hirshberg, Bellingham., *Principled Commitment*.
[188] Apostolos-Cappadonna, editor, *The Sacred Play of Children*.
[189] *Ibid.*, xi.
[190] Berryman, *Godly Play*,1.
[191] Bushnell, *Christian Nurture*. Kindle Edition Loc. 3443.
[192] *Ibid.*, Loc. 3666.
[193] Fahs, *Today's Children and Yesterday's Heritage*, 50.

Chapter Twelve. Discourse

[194] *Random House Dictionary*, 563.
[195] Fielding, *Describing Curriculum Development from the Inside Out*, 188.
[196] Hunter, *Conversations With Children*, xii.
[197] *Ibid.*, 2.

[198] *Ibid.*, 1.
[199] Davis, Haymaker, Hirshberg, Bellingham, *Principle Commitment.*, Workshop 3, Activity 3.
[200] Bohm, *On Dialogue*, 6.
[201] Berryman, *Godly Play*, 34.
[202] Hunter, *The Questioning Child and Religion*, x.
[203] Kahn, in *Quest*, February 22, 2012, 5.
[204] Moran, *Showing How*, 96.
[205] *Ibid.*, 101.
[206] *Ibid.*, 99.

Chapter Thirteen. The Centers Approach to Learning

[207] Opitz, *Learning Centers*, 13.
[208] Daniels and Bizar, *Methods That Matter*, 92.
[209] Marshall, *Opening Your Class with Learning Stations*, 16.
[210] Daniels and Bizar, 91
[211] Armstrong, *Multiple Intelligences in the Classroom*, 103-104.
[212] Middleton, *Celebrating Our Roots and Branches*, 9.
[213] Opitz, 61-63.
[214] Hollerorth, *Lesson Plans. The Haunting House*, 102.
[215] Hollerorth and Eccleston, *The Five Components of The Haunting House*, 10.
[216] Middleton, *Celebrating Our Roots and Branches*.
[217] Middleton, *Special Times*.
[218] Sautter, *A World of New Friends*.

Chapter Fourteen. Real World Experiences

[219] Daniels and Bizar. *Methods That Matter*, 171.
[220] Cathy Cartwright-Chow, personal correspondence.

Chapter Fifteen. Reflection and Meditation

[221] Developed by Elizabeth Katzmann and Meg Riley. Used with permission.
[222] www.labyrinthsociety.org.
[223] www.towardtheone.com.
[224] www.uua.org/re/tapestry.
[225] Olson and York. *Creating Home*.

[226] York. *Signs of Our Faith.*
[227] Anacheka-Nasemann and Pearmain. *Moral Tales.* Session 3.

Chapter Sixteen. Tomorrow's Children and Today's Heritage

[228] Gardner, "Multiple Approaches to Understanding," 114-115.

References

Anacheka-Nasemann, Alice, and Elisa Davy Pearmain. *Moral Tales.* www.uua.org/re/tapestry/moraltales. Accessed May 21, 2015.

Anastos, Elizabeth and David Marshak, editors. *Philosophy-Making for Unitarian Universalist Religious Growth and Learning.* Boston: Unitarian Universalist Association 1984.

Anderson, Herbert, and Edward Foley. *Mighty Stories, Dangerous Rituals. Weaving Together the Human and the Divine.* San Francisco: Jossey Bass 1998.

Andrews, Barry. "The Soul Only Avails: Teaching as a Spiritual Act," www.uuneedham.org/wp-content/uploads/2014/02/Teaching-as-a-Spiritual-Act.pdf. Accessed April 6, 2015.

Apostolos-Cappadonna, Diane, editor. *The Sacred Play of Children.* New York: Seabury Press 1983.

Archer, Susan Davison. "Outside the Box," *Essex Conversations: Visions for Lifespan Religious Education.* Essex Conversations Coordinating Committee. Boston: Skinner House 2001.

Armstrong, Thomas. *Multiple Intelligences in the Classroom* 3rd Edition. Alexandria, VA: Association for Supervision and Curriculum Development 2009.

Armstrong-Hansche, Melissa, and Neil MacQueen. *Workshop Rotation. A New Model for Sunday School.* Louisville, KY: Geneva Press 2000.

Ashton-Warner, Sylvia. *Teacher.* New York: Simon & Schuster 1963.

Bacharach, Nancy, Robin Christine Hasslen, and Jill Anderson. *Learning Together. A Manual for Multiage Grouping.* Thousand Oaks, CA: Corwin Press Inc. 1955.

Baker, Elizabeth H. *Retrospect, Unitarian Universalist Advance Study Paper No. 14 A.* Unitarian Universalist Advance 1980.

Berryman, Jerome W. *Godly Play: An Imaginative Approach to Religious Education.* Minneapolis: Augsburg 1991.

Berryman, Jerome W. *Teaching Godly Play: The Sunday Morning Handbook.* Nashville: Abingdon Press 1995.

Blumberg, Sherry. "President's Column," *REACH, Religious Education Association Clearing House,* Vol. XXIX No. 2. Decatur, GA: Religious Education Association 1999.

Bohm, David. *On Dialogue,* Lee Nichols, editor. New York: Routledge 1998.

Boys, Mary C. *Educating in Faith: Maps & Visions.* Kansas City, MO: Sheed and Ward 1989.

Brandt, Ron. *On Teaching for Understanding.* www.ascd.org/publications/educational-leadership/apr93/vol50/num07/

On-Teaching-for-Understanding@-A-Conversation-with-Howard-Gardner.aspx. Accessed April 3, 2015.

Bruner, Jerome. "Culture, Mind, and Education," *Contemporary Theories of Learning: Learning Theorists in Their Own Words.* New York: Routledge 2009.

Bumbaugh, David E. *Unitarian Universalism: A Narrative History.* Chicago: Meadville Lombard Press 2000.

Bushnell, Horace. *Christian Nurture.* New York: Scribner, Armstrong & Co. 1876. Kindle Edition.

Carson, Rachel. *The Sense of Wonder.* New York: Harper & Row 1965.

Cartwright-Chow, Cathy. Personal Correspondence, March 18, 2015.

Channing, William Ellery. *Discourse Pronounced to the Sunday School Society, The Works of William E. Channing.* Boston: American Unitarian Society 1870.

Chapman, Carolyn. *If the Shoe Fits: How to Develop Multiple Intelligences in the Classroom.* Palatine, IL: IRI/Skylight Publishing 1993.

Chase, Penelle, Jane Doan and Contributing Educators. *Full Circle: A New Look at Multiage Education.* Portsmouth, NH: Heinemann 1994.

Commission III. "Education and Liberal Religion," *The Free Church in a Changing World: The Reports of the Commissions to the Churches and Fellowships of the Unitarian Universalist Association.* Boston: Unitarian Universalist Association 1963.

Covey, Katie. *Chalice Children.* www.uua.org/re/tapestry. Accessed April 20, 2015.

Crossan, John Dominic. *The Dark Interval: Toward a Theology of Story.* Niles, IL: Argus 1975.

Crossan, John Dominic. *The Dark Interval: Toward a Theology of Story.* Revised and Corrected Edition. Sonoma, CA: Polebridge Press 1988.

Crowley, Abby L. W., editor. *Windmills, Worship, and Wonder: Ideas for Intergenerational Worship.* Adelphi MD: Greater Washington Area Religious Education Council 1996.

Crowley, Abby L. W., editor. *Together Time: A Sourcebook of Ideas for Intergenerational Worship.* Adelphi, MD: Greater Washington Area Religious Education Council 2001.

Daniels, Harvey, and Marilyn Bizar. *Methods That Matter: Six Structures for Best Practice Classrooms.* Portland, ME: Stenhouse Publishers 1998.

Davis, Melanie J., Stephanie Haymaker, Craig Hirshberg, and Richard Bellingham. *Principled Commitment.* www.uua.org/re/tapestry. Accessed April 2, 2015.

Declaration of the Rights of the Child, www.unicef.org/malaysia/1959-Declaration-of-the-Rights-of-the-Child.pdf Accessed June 1, 2015.

Dillard, Annie. *An American Childhood.* New York: Harper & Row 1987.

Elkjaer, Bente. "Pragmatism: a Learning Theory for the Future." *Contemporary Theories of Learning: Learning Theorists in Their Own Words. New York: Routledge 2009.*

Essex Conversations Coordinating Committee. *Essex Conversations.* Boston: Skinner House 2001.

Fahs, Sophia Lyon. *Today's Children and Yesterday's Heritage.* Boston: Beacon Press 1952.

Fewkes, Richard. "Theodore Parker Speaks," *The Transient and Permanent in Liberal Religion. Reflections from the UUMA Convocation on Ministry.* Boston: Skinner House 1995.

Fielding, Glen. *Describing Curriculum Development from the Inside Out, Journal of Curriculum and Supervision.* Winter 1989. Vol. 4 No. 2.

Frediani, Judith. "Making Sure There is a There There," *Essex Conversations.* Essex Conversations Coordinating Committee. Boston: Skinner House 2006.

Freire, Paulo. *A Pedagogy for the Oppressed.* New Revised 20th Anniversary Edition. New York: Continuum 1994.

www.funderstanding.com. Accessed April 14, 2015.

Galindo, Israel. *The Craft of Christian Teaching: Essentials for Becoming a Very Good Teacher.* Valley Forge, PA: Judson Press 1998.

Gardner, Howard. *Frames of Mind: The Theory of Multiple Intelligences.* Tenth Anniversary Edition. New York: Basic Books 2004.

Gardner, Howard. *Intelligence Reframed: Multiple Intelligences for the 21st Century.* New York: Basic Books 1999.

Gardner, Howard. "Multiple Approaches to Understanding," *Contemporary Theories of Learning: Learning Theorists in Their Own Words.* Knud Illeris, editor. London and New York: Routledge 2006.

Gilbert, Richard S. *Growing Up Absorbed.* Bloomington, IN: iUniverse 2014.

Gilbert, Richard S. and Roberta Nelson. *Religious Education and Social Action: Branches of the Same Tree.* Boston: Unitarian Universalist Association 1984.

Griggs, Donald, and Patricia Griggs. *Generations Learning Together.* Nashville: Abingdon 1980.

Groome, Thomas. *Christian Religious Education: Sharing Our Story and Vision.* San Francisco: Jossey-Bass 1980.

Gutek, Gerald Lee, editor. *The Montessori Method.* Lanham, MD: Rowman & Littlefield Publishers, Inc. 2004.

Harris, Sandra Gutridge. *Getting Started in Storytelling.* Indianapolis: Stonework Press 1990.

Henderson, Dorothy. *"Worship and Sunday School: Which is best for your* congregation?," The Presbyterian Church in Canada's PC Pak, February 2003.

Hollerorth, Barbara. *The Haunting House.* Boston: Unitarian Universalist Association 1974.

Hollerorth, Barbara. *Lesson Plans. The Haunting House. Building and Living in Houses.* Boston: Unitarian Universalist Association 1974.

Hollerorth, Barbara, and Helen Eccleston. *The Five Components of The Haunting House.* Boston: Unitarian Universalist Association 1974.

Hollerorth, Hugo J. "An Era of Change," *Claiming the Past, Shaping the Future,* Roberta M. Nelson, editor. Providence, RI: Liberal Religious Educators Association and Blackstone Editions 2006.

Hollerorth, Hugo J. "Focus on a New Era: The Making of a Curriculum," *The Register-Leader of the Unitarian Universalist Association.* Volume 149, Number 4. April 1967.

Hollerorth, Hugo J., editor. *Stone House Conversations.* Boston: Unitarian Universalist Association 1980.

Hunter, Edith F., *Conversations With Children.* Boston: Beacon Press 1961.

Hurd, Tracey L. *Nurturing Children and Youth: A Developmental Guidebook.* Boston: Unitarian Universalist Association 2005.

Hymnbook Resources Commission. *Singing the Living Tradition.* Boston: Unitarian Universalist Association 1994.

Illeris, Knud, editor. *Contemporary Theories of Learning: Learning Theorists in Their Own Words.* London and New York: Routledge 2009.

Jarvis, Peter. "Learning to be a Person in Society: Learning to be Me," *Contemporary Theories of Learning,* Knud Illeris, editor. London and New York: Routledge 2009.

Jarvis, Peter. *Towards a Comprehensive Theory of Human Learning.* New York: Routledge 2006.

Joyce, Bruce, and Marsha Weil, with Emily Calhoun. *Models of Teaching.* Boston: Allyn and Bacon 2002.

Kahn, Deborah. *Quest,* Newsletter of the Unitarian Universalist Church of Rockville, MD: February 22, 2012.

Kent, Corita, and Jan Steward. *Learning by Heart: Teachings to Free the Creative Spirit.* New York: Bantam Books 1992.

Kimball, Richard. *Amazing Grace. Field Test.* www.uua.org/re/tapestry. Accessed November 12, 2011.

Koch, Kenneth, and The Students of P.S. 61 in New York City. *Wishes, Lies, and Dreams: Teaching Children to Write Poetry.* New York: Vintage Books 1970.

www.learning-theories.com. Accessed August 5, 2014.

www.labyrinthsociety.org/download-a-labyrinth. Accessed May 21, 2015.

MacLean, Angus H. *The Method is the Message.* Boston: Unitarian Universalist Association 1962.

MacQueen, Neil. *The Workshop Rotation Model. A Brief Introduction and History,* www.rotation.org. Accessed April 14, 2015

Marshall, Kim. *Opening Your Class with Learning Stations.* A LEARNING Handbook. Palo Alto, CA: Education Today Company, Inc. 1975.

McLuhan, Marshall. *Understanding Media: The Extensions of Man.* Cambridge, MA: Massachusetts Institute of Technology 1994.

Mezirow, Jack, and Associates. *Learning as Transformation: Critical Perspectives on A Theory in Progress.* San Francisco: Jossey-Bass-2000.

Middleton, Betty Jo. *Celebrating Our Roots and Branches. A religious education program for children ages 5 through 8.* Lutherville, MD: Joseph Priestley District Religious Education Committee 1979.

Middleton, Betty Jo. *Special Times: Honoring Our Jewish and Christian Heritages.* Boston: Unitarian Universalist Association 1994.

Middleton, Betty Jo. "How We Do What We Do in Religious Education," *Reader for Graduate Course in Religious Education.* Betty Jo Middleton, editor. www.ibrarian.net/navon/page. jsp?paperid=8563588. 2004. Accessed February 25, 2015.

Milgrom, Jo. *Handmade Midrash: Workshops in Visual Theology.* Philadelphia, New York, Jerusalem: The Jewish Publication Society 1992.

Miller, Lisa, Ph.D. *The Spiritual Child: The New Science on Parenting for Health and Lifelong Thriving.* New York: St. Martin's Press 2015.

Moran, Gabriel. *Religious Education as a Second Language.* Birmingham, AL: Religious Education Press 1989.

Moran, Gabriel. *Religious Education Development: Images for the Future.* Minneapolis: Winston Press 1983.

Moran, Gabriel. *Showing How. The Act of Teaching.* Valley Forge, PA: Trinity Press International 1997.

Murray, Judith Sargent Stevens. *A Universalist Catechism.* Cambridge, MA: Judith Sargent Murray Society 1999.

Navias, Eugene B. "The Fourth Level of Teaching," *Checkpoints for Teachers.* Boston: Unitarian Universalist Association 1977.

Navias, Eugene B. "A Short History of Unitarian Universalist Religious Education," *Reader for Graduate Course in Religious Education.* Betty Jo Middleton, editor. 2004. www.ibrarian.net/ navon/page.jsp?paperid=8563588. Accessed April 3, 2015.

Navias, Eugene B. "Two Contrasting Philosophies of Religious Education," *Introduction to Liberal Religious Education: A Graduate Level Course for Unitarian Universalists.* 2004. www.uua/org/publications/middleton/betty. Accessed November 10, 2011.

Nelson, Roberta M. "The Teacher as Spiritual Guide," *Essex Conversations.* Essex Conversations Coordinating Committee. Boston: Skinner House 2001.

Nelson, Roberta M., editor. *Claiming the Past. Shaping the Future.* Providence, RI: Liberal Religious Educators Association and Blackstone Editions 2006.

Neville, Gwen Kennedy. "Cultural and Community Roots of Liturgy," *Learning Through Liturgy.* New York: Seabury Press 1978.

www.nifply.org. Accessed April 3, 2015.

Nieuwejaar, Jeanne H. *The Gift of Faith.* Boston: Skinner House 1999.

Nieuwejaar, Jeanne H. "The Early Years. 1790-1930," *Claiming the Past. Shaping the Future.* Roberta M. Nelson, editor. Providence, RI: Liberal Religious Educators Association and Blackstone Editions 2006.

www.npr.org/blogs/ed/2014/08/06/336360521/play-doesn't-end-with-childhood-why-adults-need-recess-too. Accessed March 18, 2015.

O'Donnell, Mickie, and Vickie Dare. *Workshop Wonders: The Ultimate Guide to Rotation Sunday School.* Colorado Springs, CO: Cook Communication Ministries 2005.

Olson, Christy, and Jessica York. *Creating Home.* www.uua.org/re/ tapestrychildren/home. Accessed April 20, 2015.

O'Neal, Dan, Alice Blair Wesley, and James Ishmael Ford, editors. *The Transient and Permanent in Liberal Religion. Reflections from the UUMA Convocation on Ministry.* Boston: Skinner House 1995.

Opitz, Michael F. *Learning Centers: Getting Them Started, Keeping Them Going.* New York: Scholastic Professional Books 1994.

Ostrow, Jill. *A Room With a Different View. First Through Third Graders Build Community and Create Curriculum.* York, ME: Stenhouse Publishers 1995.

Palmer, Parker J. *The Courage to Teach: Exploring the Inner Landscape of a Teacher's Life.* San Francisco: Jossey-Bass 1998.

Parke, David B. *The Children Were My Teachers: The Revolution in Religious Education.* Chicago: Meadville Lombard Press 2009.

Parker, Theodore. *A Discourse of Matters Pertaining to Religion.* 1842.

Parker, Theodore. "The Transient and Permanent in Christianity," *Three Prophets of Religious Liberalism,* edited by Conrad Wright. Boston: Beacon Press 1964.

Patton, Sally. *Welcoming Children With Special Needs.* Boston: Unitarian Universalist Association 2004.

Peebles, Linda Olson. "Lessons from a Tube of Toothpaste," in *Windmills, Worship, and Wonder: Ideas for Intergenerational Worship.* Adelphi MD: Greater Washington Area Religious Education Council 1996.

Penfold, Nita. *Spirit Play: A Manual for Liberal Religious Education Programs.* Self published 2008.

The Random House Dictionary of the English Language. Second Edition. Unabridged. New York: Random House 1997.

Religious Education Futures Committee. *Report to the Unitarian Universalist Association Board of Trustees.* Boston: Unitarian Universalist Association 1981.

Robertson, Frank E. "The Fahs/MacLean Era," *Claiming the Past, Shaping the Future: Four Eras in Liberal Religious Education 1790-1999.* Roberta M. Nelson, editor. Providence, RI: Liberal Religious Education Association and Blackstone Editions 2006.

Robinson, Edward. *The Original Vision: A Study of the Religious Experience of Childhood.* New York: Seabury Press 1983.

Sautter, Sara L. *A World of New Friends: An Introduction to World Religions.* Lenexa, KS: Shawnee Mission Unitarian Universalist Church 2004.

Schulte, Brigid. *Overwhelmed: Work, Love, and Play When No One Has the Time.* New York: Farrar, Strauss and Giroux 2014.

Searle, Mark. "Preface," *The Religious Potential of the Church, The Religious Potential of the Child*, by Sofia Cavaletti. Mt. Ranier, MD: Association of the Catechesis Of the Good Shepherd 1992.

Simon, Sidney B. and Merrill Harmin, *Subject Matter With a Focus on Values.* www.ascd.org/publications/educational/leadership/oct68/vol26/num01/toc/aspx. Accessed June 1, 2015.

Stewart, Greg. "Sunday School is Dead. Long Live Sunday School." *Essex Conversations: Visions for Lifespan Religious Education.* Essex Conversations Coordinating Committee. Boston: Skinner House 2001.

www.spirit-play.com. Accessed November 2, 2014.

Spoerl, Dorothy Tilden. *The Creative Process and Religious Education.* Boston: Unitarian Universalist Association, Horizon Series Number One 1994.

Strong, Elizabeth M. *The Larger Message: Universalist Religious Education's Response to Cultural Challenges 1790–1999.* Chicago: Meadville Lombard Press 2004.

Strong, Elizabeth M. "Synopsis of Unitarian Universalist Religious Education Eras," from a lecture given at Murray Grove Conference Center 2014.

Strong, Elizabeth M. "The Rise of the Sunday School Movement," lecture given at Murray Grove Conference Center 2014.

Tolley, John W. "Child's Play," *Essex Conversations.* Boston: Skinner House 2001.

Unitarian Universalist Association. *Singing the Living Tradition.* Boston: Beacon Press 1994.

www.towardtheone.com/sufidance/about/html

www.uua.org/re/tapestry. Accessed December 1, 2014.

www.uua.org/re/teachers/webinars. Accessed November 14, 2014.

Wesley, Alice Blair. *Myths of Time and History: A Unitarian Universalist Theology.* Self published 1987.

White, James W. *Intergenerational Religious Education.* Birmingham, AL: Religious Education Press 1988.

Wiske, Martha Stone, editor. *Teaching for Understanding: Linking Research With Practice.* San Francisco: Jossey-Bass 1998.

Wolf, Aline D. *Nurturing the Spirit in Non-Sectarian Classrooms.* Holidaysburg, PA: Parent Child Press 1996.

Abbreviations

ASCD	Association of Curriculum and Development
AUA	American Unitarian Association
AYS	About Your Sexuality
CLF	Church of the Larger Fellowship
COA	Coming of Age
GWAREC	Greater Washington Religious Education Council (or Cluster)
JPD	Joseph Priestley District of the Unitarian Universalist Association
LREDA	Liberal Religious Educators Association
OWL	Our Whole Lives
REA	Religious Education Association
SGM	Small Group Ministry
UCA	Universalist Church of America
UU	Unitarian Universalist or Unitarian Universalism
UUA	Unitarian Universalist Association
UUCARDS	Unitarian Universalist Curriculum and Resource Developers
UUCF	Unitarian Universalist Christian Fellowship
USSS	Unitarian Sunday School Society
YRUU	Young Religious Unitarian Universalists

Index

Printed in the United States
By Bookmasters